THE ENCOURAGING HEARTS HANDBOOK

A study guide and discussion questions are available for this book at: www.GreatFriendships.com

Linda Evans Shepherd is a national speaker and may be available for your next retreat or special event. Contact Linda online at www.GotToPray.com

To Millie

The Encouraging Hearts Handbook

How to be a Good Friend

Linda Shepherd

Enjoy God's gift of friends!

BVB

Bold Vision Books
PO Box 2011
Friendswood, Texas 77549

Love, Linda Evans Shepherd

ISBN: 978-0-9912842-1-4
Library of Congress Control No: 2013957404
Bold Vision Books
PO Box 2011
Friendswood, Texas 77549

Published in association with Books and Such Literary Agency, 5926 Sunhawk Drive, Santa Rosa, CA 95409.
Printed in the United States of America.

The names and characterizations originating in this book are fictional, although based on real events. Any similarity between the names or characterizations and real people is unintended and purely coincidental.

In loving memory of my grandmother,
Sue Leland Davis Aldrich
1906–1997

She was an outstanding Bible teacher
who dedicated her life to her family
and to her Lord and Savior.

Acknowledgments

Special thanks to all who contributed their wonderful stories and insights to this project, including:

Alene Betts,
Kathy Collard Miller,
Mary Evans,
Rona Peace,
Lynne Beaulieu,
Linda Deeming,
Kathy Zlomke,
Pat Drotar,
Sharon Shepherd,
Dorothy Weatherly,
Mel Tunney,
Vickie Kraft,
Louie Cordileone,
Deborah Rice,
Susan Titus Osborn,
Lynette Pickering,
Kathy Howe,
Janet Laurel,
Carolyn Scheidies,
Pam Bianco,
Mimi Deeths,
Karen O'Connor,
Verna Evans,
Barb McCauley,
Becky McMurdo,
Avonne Kettler,
Dorothy Ericson,
Lois Youree,
Glenna Salsbury,
Karen Bengtson,
Shan Darling,
LeAnn Thieman,
Joe Sabah
Penny Prater,
Debbie Barker,
and many others.
Dianne E. Butts,
Diana James,
Bonnie Skinner,
Rose Sweet,
Carey Hovestol,
Lynda Atwood,
Grace Buller,
Janelle Prante,
Corinne Bergstrom,
Kim Camp,
Conni Reed,
Lori Brunet,
Connie Neumann,
Sharon Williams,
Kathleen Pace Osborn,
Nancy Franz,
Donna Rae Manzanares,

Your wonderful insights have enriched not only my heart, but the hearts of my readers. Thank you for your contributions and help.

Table of Contents

One

Encourage Me

We drove toward home, hoping to beat the approaching darkness as shadows stretched down the city street. As our rusty pickup rattled over a small bridge, we noticed an elderly woman standing near the rail. Her head was down and her eyes squeezed shut as she gripped her walker as if to brace against the evening's chill. Something's wrong, I thought.

We doubled back to get a better look and as we slowed down I could see that one leg of the woman's walker was caught in a crack in the pavement. She was too feeble to pull it out and if someone didn't help soon, she looked as if she would collapse in the night air.

I brought the truck to a stop and my thirteen-year-old friend, Chris, hopped out. The frightened look on the old woman's face told me she thought we were robbers. That is, until Chris gently pulled her walker leg out of the crack and set her free.

I called, "Do you need a ride?"

"I'm almost home," she said.

Chris and I made sure of that as we circled the block once again and watched her hobble into her house, two doors down. The woman didn't need a ride; she needed a hand because a crack in the pavement had stalled her journey. Most of us can relate to that.

How many times have you been stuck in a rut? How many times have you fallen through a crack in your life's journey?

Trapped in life's pitfalls, you need a tug, a push, a gentle reminder to keep trying. You need the hand of a friend.

That's the beauty of encouragement. It provides a way to go on despite life's hazards. Not only do we need to receive this gift, we also need to give it. Here, in these pages, you'll find an intimate peek at encouragement, along with practical ways to become encouraged yourself.

A Wing on the Way

"There are people who take the heart out of you," said Elizabeth David, "and there are people who put it back." God has called us to restore the hearts of others: "Therefore encourage one another and build each other up, just as in fact you are doing" (1 Thes 5:11).

What is encouragement? The New Expanded Webster's Dictionary defines it like this: "To give courage to; to stimulate; to embolden; to countenance."

I would add that encouragement means to give wings. Too many women are trying to fly with broken wings of discouragement. One young mother told me, "I had a horrible day. Then, when my husband came home, he commented on the messy house and asked why I hadn't started supper yet. He was off duty, but I was evidently still on duty with the house, dinner, and kids. His comment really hurt. It would have helped so much if he had just pitched in."

Lydia, a stay-at-home mom, felt hurt when a friend she admired made her feel guilty and lazy. "I told her I was taking a break from working outside the home so I could concentrate on my family," Lydia said. "My friend asked, 'Did you win the lottery or are you going to let your husband support you?' I felt defensive and small in her eyes."

It seems we can't win. While Lydia felt discouraged by her friend for staying home with her children, Sara felt discouraged for working outside her home. She said, "I was going through a hard time financially when a friend told me I shouldn't be working. She said I was abandoning my kids. That really hurt. How I wish my friend would have supported me. It would have helped if she'd canned the criticism and given me laundry tips and organizational ideas so I could take better advantage of the time I did have."

Rehydrating Hearts

Have you ever seen foil packets of freeze-dried beef stew? Discouragement is a lot like the process that shrivels a perfectly good meal into powder. Happily, this process can be reversed. If you add water and heat the dehydrated stew, you will enjoy a warm meal.

Encouragement is like the water and warmth that reconstitutes freeze-dried stew. If you don't add it to your circumstances, you'll be in danger of drying up and blowing away.

I'm amazed at how little encouragement the average woman receives nowadays. She often finds her struggles greater, workloads heavier, grief more frequent and life more isolated than did women who came before. She's looking for someone to come alongside, to inspire her and reconstitute her dreams. Life may still be difficult, but encouragement may be the ingredient a woman needs to turn disappointments into achievements.

Recycle Courage

If you've ever been on the receiving end of encouragement, you know how valuable it can be. A few years ago, I was a discouraged writer. I'd sent my manuscripts to publishing houses across the country only to have many of the world's finest editors recycled my work back to my mailbox in large, coffin-like envelopes. Depressed, I cried out to God, "I thought you called me to write. Did I hear wrong? Should I quit?"

God's call to write remained strong so I kept sending my work into the world and continued to collect rejections. In a few months' time, my 'rejection slip' shoe box overflowed with more than two hundred 'no-thank-yous.' I called my friend Marcia, who lives two thousand miles away, just so she could comfort me with her condolences. "Marcia, I don't think I can go on," I whined. "These rejections hurt too much. I've finally reached my limit. I don't think I'll ever write again."

Marcia barked a laugh. "I know you," she said in her Bostonian way. "You'll never quit writing and one day I'll be able to say, 'I knew you when you were a nobody!' I'm going to call you on the phone and say, 'Do you remember when you said you'd never write again?' We'll laugh about this. You'll see."

I was disappointed in Marcia. I'd wanted sympathy but she'd given me a gentle push at the base of my spine. Although her chuckles jarred my crushed ego, my hope was ignited. Later, a beautiful china teapot arrived in the mail with a note from Marcia saying: "When you publish your next book, brew a cup of tea and call me. We'll have a party."

I felt blessed. Not only did my friend believe in me, she cared enough to encourage me. Now, thirty books later, Marcia and I have shared many a cup of tea and many a laugh over my threat to quit writing. How grateful I am her words and actions helped make a difference in my life!

Encourage Others

It's too bad you and I don't always have a Marcia in our lives when we need one. Sometimes that longed-for encouragement is difficult to find. In fact, I've often found I need to be the first to give encouragement to someone else. When I do, I find this gift to be the very thing that, sooner or later, regenerates my own soul.

Just as you cannot give a rose without being blessed by its fragrance, you cannot give encouragement without being encouraged. This was true in a season of grief in Jane's life. Her husband suffers from complications of diabetes and she has health problems of her own.

"I have always been the one to encourage others," she told me. "After Ned's operation on his feet, I got depressed. But the friends I've encouraged over the years began to encourage me. People wrote, 'Jane, you don't know how much you've helped me. I want to thank you for that.'"

Jane smiled and pulled a tissue from her purse. "I'm a firm believer in that saying, 'What goes around, comes around.' Now that I'm a senior citizen, it is gratifying to know that the investments I made in the lives of others have been compounding with interest."

What It's All About

Jane's ability to uplift others reminds me of the lesson my parents taught me as a child: "Always try to find something nice to say about someone else."

I took those words to heart. When I was a second-grader, I studied my girlfriends, looking for something nice to say. Some days it wasn't easy. I remember desperately searching for a compliment to give one forlorn seven-year-old. She was wearing a wrinkled cotton shift and her hair hung in strings. I didn't want to lie, but I had to say something to cheer her. Then I noticed she wore buckled dress shoes instead of tennis shoes. (At my house, patent-leather shoes were reserved only for Sundays.) Although little Sheila's patent-leathers were so scuffed I could barely see any shine, I blurted, "I like your shoes."

Sheila looked down at her scuffed, hand-me-down patent-leathers, then back at me. Though she knew her shoes were worn, she recognized I was trying to be her friend. She smiled and we joined hands, skipping to the blacktop to play hopscotch.

I don't know what your shoes look like, but because you're holding this book in your hands, I know you're a real angel, a person who longs not just to have a friend, but to be a friend and give others wings.

An old Chinese proverb says,

> If your vision is for a year, plant wheat.
> If your vision is for ten years, plant trees.
> If your vision is for a lifetime, plant people.

Encouragers plant people. Their efforts mean they will reap a harvest. Get ready to sow and to be sown into the lives of others as an encourager.

Two

We Need Each Other

One day, I was scanning a friend's magnet-covered Frigidaire when I came across this quotation: "We are like angels with just one wing. We fly only by embracing each other."

What a mental picture. When you think about it, you can imagine that a one-winged angel could beat his wing all day and never achieve liftoff. But by combining forces with another one-winged angel, the pair has the ability to fly.

My friend Connie can relate and told me how one of her friends came alongside to help her soar. She said, "My friend was like an angel unaware. I doubt she realizes how much her support helped."

"What happened?" I asked.

"I'm a librarian at an elementary school," Connie said. "When I got a degree in library science, I never dreamed my job would include working with computers and the Internet." She sighed. "But I don't have the budget I need and my computers are always on the blink. One day I got so frustrated, I decided this was not how I wanted to spend my life and that I should quit.

"That's when another teacher stopped by my desk and asked, 'May I encourage you?'

"I couldn't believe she used those words." Connie swallowed hard. "I told her about my struggles. She listened and encouraged me to keep going. My problems did not go away, but because of her, I did not resign."

Connie had been flapping one wing furiously for months, only to find herself earthbound. The words of a friend gave her the lift she needed to continue. Those words didn't change Connie's circumstances, but they enabled her to rise above them.

Women today need each other more than ever before.

We need mentoring and encouragement.

We need to avoid the pitfalls of codependency.

We need tips for acquiring and building relationships.

Women Mentor Women

I love to go online and join discussion groups and have enjoyed the opportunity to share instant messaged conversations with people from all over the world. Recently, a man joined a conversation with me and about fifteen other Christian women speakers. He typed, "Linda, you're wrong to be teaching. Women should be silent! Can you show me one place in Scripture where it says women should teach?"

I smiled, my fingers flying as I typed, "Try Titus 2:3-5. It is one of the few commands directed just to women: 'Likewise, teach the older women to be reverent in the way they live, not to be slanderers or addicted to much wine, but to teach what is good. Then they can train the younger women to love their husbands and children, to be self-controlled and pure, to be busy at home, to be kind, and to be subject to their husbands, so that no one will malign the word of God.'"

Funny thing—my challenger dropped the subject. Why? Because Scripture is clear, women need to mentor women. Think about it: a husband can't affirm a woman in all the roles of her life. He hasn't walked in her shoes, had a baby and most likely hasn't been married to a man, so he can't possibly understand how to counsel her in those areas.

Vickie Kraft, author of Women Mentoring Women, told me, "Most women have been raised by a woman, so female relationships are very normal. Plus, women need to have someone with whom to express their thoughts and feelings. The average man is not going to meet all a woman's emotional and relational needs. He may try, but he isn't equipped."

Only a woman can put her arm around another and assure her by saying, "That same thing happened to me, too and I lived through it. You're going to make it too."

That's credibility. It's heartening when we draw on the wisdom of those who have gone before.

Recently, I was in a position to share my time-earned wisdom with a younger woman from Oceanside. We went out for breakfast and talked about spiritual things like finding God's will. Since Jenni was expecting, we also talked about babies, raising children and (you guessed it) labor and delivery!

Jenni was nervous. She asked questions like, "What if I have a hard labor? Is it going to be very painful? How am I going to make it through?"

As a mother of two, I told Jenni, "Even if your labor is hard, when you hold that baby in your arms for the first time, it will all be worth it."

She needed to hear that from someone who had experienced it. Later, she said those words kept her going during the twelve difficult hours that led to the birth of her precious daughter.

Say No to Controlling Relationships

Encouraging other women can have its pitfalls also. The biggest thing to guard against is the danger of codependency which is relying on a human relationship more than relying on God. This means we must constantly challenge our friends to depend upon the Lord instead of upon us.

Rose was in a codependent friendship for thirty years with Betty, an older woman who manipulated her. Betty told Rose how to dress, what to buy and what to do. Rose always went along with Betty's wishes for fear of losing her friendship. One day, Betty demanded that Rose divulge a secret about a mutual friend whose husband was caught in an affair. Rose wouldn't tell the secret because she knew Betty could never keep the juicy tale to herself.

Betty pleaded, threatened and used guilt to try to make Rose talk. Yet Rose held her silence and met her worst fear head-on—Betty terminated their friendship.

Although Rose felt bad about the break, God eventually brought new friends into her life. Looking back several years later, Rose is glad she resisted the temptation to gossip. She feels sorry Betty won't speak to her, yet she's relieved to be free from Betty's control.

In friendship, manipulation and control are wrong. But how do you know if your friendships are out of bounds. For starters, ask yourself; Do I have a friend who needs me to tell her what to do? Do I feel she can't brush her teeth without my help?

If so, stop playing games. Point your friend toward God, not yourself. Let her make her own decisions as well as her own mistakes. I'm not saying it's wrong to encourage her or to share your opinions with her, but it is wrong to allow yourself to be her all-in-all or in other words, it's wrong for you to allow yourself to be her god.

Another question to ask yourself is; Do I have a friend who is controlling me? Am I afraid she'll withhold friendship if I don't jump through her every hoop?

If so, prayerfully consider whether you should continue your jumping routine. Refusal to jump may cause you to lose a friend, but it may allow you to regain your freedom in God.

When should you go against your friend's wishes or opinions? First, pray. Ask God to show you what to do. If he leads you to take a stand, prayerfully and lovingly explain your decision to your friend. If she breaks the friendship, God may lead you to new friends whom you might not have gotten a chance to know otherwise.

But regardless, the bottom line is this: you can't let the fear of abandonment keep you from doing what you know is right.

I understand the fear of abandonment. When my daughter, Laura, was eighteen months old, she and I were in a car accident that left her in a coma for a year. When she woke up, severely disabled and on life support, we continued to supply round-the-clock care for her in our home.

Eunice worked the night shift. Sometimes I would find her asleep beside Laura's bed. When I told Eunice she had to stay awake when caring for my daughter, she promised to shape up, then reminded me how hard she'd be to replace. Although I continued to be unhappy with Eunice's work, she convinced me that I had no choice but to employ her.

One night, Eunice treated my daughter in a very negligent way. I did what was right: I let her go. Now what am I going to do? I worried as Eunice walked out of my door for the last time. Quickly, I asked God for help and he came through. Within a week, I had a care-giver who loved helping my daughter in the evenings. I lost one helper but gained a new, more loving one.

The point is we shouldn't allow threats to keep us in a bad relationship. When we pray it through and move in the way God leads, he provides.

Making New Friends

There comes a time in everyone's life when he or she needs to make new friends. A few years ago, I looked around and found most of my closest friends had either moved to California or divorced and moved in other directions. One friend invited me to meet her at the local pancake house. I was surprised when she confided, "I have a new lover and I'm getting rid of everything in my life that reminds me of the past." She paused and looked me in the eyes. "I'm sorry to say, Linda, that includes our friendship."

This friend was only one of many who walked out of my life after the car accident. It seemed so many of these dear-ones no longer saw me as a person but as a tragedy. They'd put on their most doleful faces and use their most mournful voices to ask, "How are you? How's little Laura?"

While I was grateful for their concern and prayers, I was lonely for their friendship. No one wanted to talk about normal things or spend time with me because my circumstance depressed them. My phone stopped ringing and my dinner invitations were turned down. My husband and I made the decision to try to build new friendships with other couples because we understood the importance of finding good friends. It's like the writer of Ecclesiastes explained:

> Two are better than one, because they have a good return for their work: If one falls down, his friend can help him up. But pity the man who falls and has no one to help him up! Also, if two lie down together, they will keep warm.

But how can one keep warm alone? Though one may be overpowered, two can defend themselves. "A cord of three strands is not quickly broken" (Ecclesiastes 4:9-12)

The Quilting Bee

Most women today are torn in so many directions that they don't have time to visit, talk on the phone or do lunch, much less make a new friend. But I found my attempts at friendship building were worth the effort because the strength gained from making a friend doubles with each new friend. Our grandmothers and their mothers knew this secret and the evidence they left behind is comforting.

Although my Grandmother Evans died when I was only five, I often snuggled beneath her beautiful pink and ivory Sunbonnet Sue quilt when I visited her farmhouse. I remember lying on the sofa bed, listening to the fire crackling in the cast-iron fireplace. Sleepily, I would stare up at two large hooks fastened into the ceiling, trying to imagine what they were for. One day, I asked my dad.

He answered, "Those were your grandmother's quilting hooks. Back in the days of the Depression, my mother and her friends gathered here. They hung a quilt from the ceiling so they could stitch and chat."

I loved to envision that scene. I pictured the front room filled with ladies in cotton calico shifts, cutting floral flour-sack fabric into the pieces of a beautiful quilt. I imagined them lovingly stitching their quilts by hand as they created their colorful masterpieces.

Though my grandmother lived in the country and didn't own a telephone, she connected with other women through her quilting bees, daylong church socials and revival meetings. Those occasions allowed her and her friends to encourage one another as they told their life stories while they worked. The older women told about the times they had made it through life's hard places. The younger women listened, gathering wisdom and advice.

What a beautiful thing the quilting bee must have been. Not only did it produce a legacy of heirloom quilts, it also produced deep friendships, allowing women to be involved in each other's lives.

Gone are the days of quilting bees, replaced by so much isolation. Today it seems that instead of spending time with the neighbors, our radio and television keeps us company. These electronic voices make poor friends and even worse mentors. But though we are often lonely, we are also busier. Many of us work outside our homes so we'll have enough money to purchase time-saving appliances like washing machines, dryers and the electricity to run them. Plus, instead of wearing a shirt five days in a row, like our grandparents did, we have to earn enough money to purchase a closet full of shirts so we'll have something to wear between washings.

So between working, shopping, managing our homes and running kids to soccer practice, we skimp on our time with friends.

I understand loneliness. When I joined a new church, I cheerfully smiled at the women I met and sometimes shared a comment or two. They seemed nice enough, but I felt frustrated. They knew little about me and I knew even less about them. We were all so busy that we never had time to visit during the week or to encourage one other. So, I began to plot. How could I capture that fellowship my grandmother had found in her quilting bees? I wondered.

I looked at the beautiful teapot Marcia had sent me. Could I host a tea for the ladies I wanted to get to know better? If we got together, how could I keep the mix of women from stumbling at small talk? How could I turn the small talk into encouragement?

Meanwhile, as I contemplated this dilemma, I decided to host a baby shower for one of the women who helped care for my daughter, hopping the party would help develop our relationships. When the women arrived for the shower, I suddenly realized I hadn't planned any party games to break the ice and wondered how I could encourage meaningful conversation.

When everyone was seated, I picked up a present covered in bunnies and topped with a pink bow. I said, "When Lisa opens your present, tell her a baby story."

"A baby story?" Sharon asked.

"You know, a story about a baby. It can be funny or practical. It can be about one of your own babies or a story about when you were a baby."

Soon we were all sharing wonderful stories of new babies and baby adventures. It seemed each story sparked another. As I looked around the room, I realized what had happened. We weren't just telling stories; we were encouraging one another with our experiences! Experienced moms were, in effect, telling the younger moms, "You're not the only one. This has happened to me too!"

I saw looks of relief on the faces of younger mothers. I saw the joy of sharing on the faces of the older mothers. Later, as I washed cake crumbs off my china plates, I thought about the camaraderie the stories had generated. I wondered, Is this the secret to building relationships? Is this how women nurture one another? If so, when I invite my church friends to tea, I need to ask them to bring their life stories.

The next day, I sat at my desk, opened a copy of the church directory and began to make a list of the ladies I would invite to my home. There were many wonderful women to choose from. I settled on women of a variety of ages and occupations. When I called to invite them to tea, each one asked, "Is there anything I can bring?"

"Yes," I replied. "I'll supply the mint tea and coffeecake. You bring a story about a time someone encouraged you."

I circled the date on my calendar. I couldn't wait to see what would happen at my Encourage Mint Tea! I hoped it could be a start to deeper friendships for us all.

THREE

ENCOURAGE MINT TEA

The morning of my tea party dawned cold and snowy. Oh no! I thought. The phone will surely ring with cancellations. To my surprise it stayed quiet. I set the dining room table with my crocheted, ivory-colored tablecloth and gold-rimmed china. I put my warm coffeecake on a platter and turned on the teakettle. Nervously, I glanced at the falling snow. Would the ladies brave the storm?

When the doorbell began to ring, I stayed busy, gathering snow-dusted coats and leading women to my kitchen. My guests seemed a little nervous but were soon laughing and chatting with one another. When everyone arrived, I invited the group to the table and poured mint tea from my floral teapot.

As we sipped tea and munched coffeecake, I said, "The reason I asked you here is because I see you at church and I enjoy talking to you, but I feel there is much more to know and love. I want you to have more input into my life and I want to have more input into your lives. I feel we need each other."

"I agree," Kathy said, while everyone nodded.

I continued, "As you know, we're going to tell stories about the times we've been encouraged. Who would like to go first?"

Connie, a senior citizen with snappy blue eyes and white curls, volunteered. She said, "I was surprised Linda invited an old bag like me to her party. I didn't know if I should come. But here I am and here's the story I want to share."

The other women and I leaned back in our chairs to listen.

"Years ago, I took care of a foster child in our home," Connie started. "When the foster child left, I felt lost. I decided to go back to school and earn a teaching degree. But I was in my thirties and wasn't sure I should be doing that. Then one of my professors took the time to bolster me with several talks. One day, he assigned a thesis. I wrote about how I had lost seventy pounds. The professor corrected some of my punctuation mistakes, then wrote a big red A+ on my paper with the note, 'I enjoyed every bite!'

"That motivated me to continue with my studies to become a teacher, a job I enjoyed thoroughly before retiring a few years ago."

Louie said, "Your professor helped you see that your work and experience were worthy."

Connie took a deep breath, then turned to Lori, a young mother of three. "I've done my part. Now it's your turn."

Lori laughed and reached for her Bible and motioned to me. "When Linda told me the theme of the party, I knew immediately what I would share." She pulled back her long black hair, then continued. “When I graduated from college and had no marriage prospects in sight, I was lonely and prayed often for a husband. I went on a mission trip to Africa but was in a panic, wondering if I were going to be an old maid.”

The other women chuckled.

Lori continued, “In Africa, one of my friends sat me down for a talk. She revitalized me with a Scripture.” Lori flipped through her Bible, then read Psalm 27:14: “‘Wait for the Lord; be strong and take heart and wait for the Lord.’” Her eyes met ours. “Those words helped me relax. I was able to realize it was all in God’s time. I continued my work in Africa and I never would have had that adventure if I had been married. When I came home, the Lord arranged for me to meet Steve.” Lori smiled. “So at the ripe old age of twenty-seven, I got married.”

We all beamed, thinking Steve, Lori and the boys made such a wonderful family.

Lori added, “When my friend shared that Scripture, it seemed like such a little thing. But it turned my thinking around and I was able to wait on God.”

“Sometimes it’s the little things that make a big difference,” Connie said.

“Yes,” I agreed. “God is faithful to use the smallest details and the kindness of others to help us through struggles.”

The group murmured their consensus. Lori closed her Bible, then looked expectantly at our other friend Lynda.

Lynda, whose hair remains dark despite the fact she has teens under her roof, leaned closer to the table. Her voice turned to a whisper. “The Lord has truly been my encourager,” she said, gathering strength to continue. “When I was twelve, my dad died of cancer. My mom had to go to work and I was left to raise myself. The Scripture that says God is a father to the fatherless was true in my life” (see Ps 68:5).

Lynda gave us a wistful smile. "Whenever I thought about getting into something I shouldn't, it was like God whispered in my ear, 'Do you really want to do that?'

"I'd say 'no,' and stop." Her eyes twinkled. "His voice kept me from getting into trouble. God has reassured me in my decision to be a stay-at-home mom. He has helped me get to the place where I'm today."

Louie's energetic voice interrupted. "I'm going crazy!" she said. "My Carrieanna is just learning to drive. She's such a sweet girl, but I'm having trouble letting go of the keys." She put her hands to her cheeks and squealed, "I'm just not ready for this!"

We laughed and Kathy patted Louie's arm. "But Carrieanna is such a responsible girl," she assured her. "She'll be a careful driver."

"I know it," Louie answered. "She drives like a little old lady. I've got to let go and encourage her more. We have only two more years together before she goes to college."

Cringing, Louie continued. "Still, I nag her. I think of my mother, nagging me." Her voice rose. "'What do you think you're doing? If you go to that concert, don't ever come home!' Now, as I look back at it, I know my mother's heart was saying, 'Be careful. I don't want anything to happen to you.' That's just not how it sounded. My father was the one who encouraged me. If I dug a ditch, he'd run over and say, 'My Louie dug that ditch. That's the best ditch I've ever seen!' In some ways it was hard to deal with his praise."

I asked, "Because you had to live up to it?"

"Exactly. But I was an A student and I got put in an accelerated class. My mom told me, 'It's not because you're smart. It's because the teacher liked you.' That stung."

Louie's voice softened. "When my mom and dad celebrated their fiftieth wedding anniversary, my brother and I had a party for them and made a beautiful memory book. Five years later, when my mom died, I went back to her house. I found little things tucked away here and there that told me she loved me. I came across a box that said, 'For the future.'"

Louie's eyes brimmed with tears. "I found the memory book my brother and I had made. A note from Mom said my brother and I should save it to use at our own golden wedding anniversaries. That's the moment I realized how much my mother loved me."

We all reached for our napkins. "That was a beautiful story," I said, dabbing my eyes. "It makes me realize how important it is to encourage my own children."

Louie raised her eyebrows. "It's difficult sometimes."

Lynda added, "I agree. Sometimes you don't know what to do. I love my teens, pray a lot and do the best I can."

Kathy nodded. "That's right. I've had to learn that with each of my four kids."

"Kathy," I asked, "are you ready to tell us your story?"

"OK," she said, taking a deep breath. "My mother died recently too. She came from strong Nebraska stock. She and Dad owned a ranch and she had a strong work ethic. I remember how she always bustled about."

Kathy's face darkened. "While Mom was visiting me, she had a massive stroke that affected her brain stem. I sat by her hospital bed and cried. She couldn't even open her eyes. It was hard to see this strong woman look helpless. Later, one of my friends brought me an afghan with a card that said, 'Just remember, when you're all alone, your loving heavenly Father is there to wrap his arms around you.' She told me whenever I felt afraid or lonely, I should wrap myself in the afghan to remind me of God wrapping me in his arms of love."

Kathy's voice quivered. "I spent so much time wrapped in that afghan, sitting near my mother's bed. I realized God was near." She looked up. "I was moved by the outpouring of love from my church family. When I would get home from the hospital, there would be a meal on the table, ready to eat. If it hadn't been for them, my family wouldn't have eaten. I wouldn't have eaten. Cooking dinner was the last thing I had on my mind.

"Now, when a friend is going through a crisis and someone says to me, 'All I can do is bring a meal,' I say, 'Do you have any idea how much that can mean? If that's all you can do, then do it.'"

"Kathy," I said, "your friend's gift of the afghan was a wonderful thing." I paused, trying to swallow the lump in my throat. "Since it's my turn to share," I continued, "I'd like to tell you how discouraged I was after my daughter's accident. If it had resulted in death, I would have received an outpouring of love like Kathy received. But Laura was in a coma for a whole year. At first, I didn't notice the silence from my church friends because I was so caught up in grief and in my new pregnancy. About the time Jimmy was born, my husband and I thought we should let our friends know we were ready to return to the world of the living. On three occasions, we asked couples to come to our house for dinner. Each time, they called to cancel."

"You mean they didn't show?" Louie asked.

"That's right," I answered. "Once, dinner had been on the table for twenty minutes by the time the husband called to say his wife couldn't stop crying. I finally understood my friends couldn't deal with our situation."

I continued, "It was difficult not to feel rejected. We finally came to realize it was time to try attending a new church."

I looked at the women seated around me. "It was such a relief when we walked in and you treated us like everyone else. You didn't know about our daughter.

"One day, I made the decision to bring Laura and her care-giver to church with us. I held my breath, waiting to see what would happen. We found seats near the back of the sanctuary. After the service, several people stopped to visit. An emotionally handicapped woman made an immediate bond with our daughter. Her example opened the way for others. We began to feel acceptance."

Connie interrupted: "Linda, what made you think we didn't know who you were?"

I stopped, stunned. "You mean, you knew all along and still treated me like I was normal? You've just encouraged me!"

When I had collected myself, I said, "What happened here today is wonderful. I have gotten to know each of you in a deeper way. I'm glad we've had this opportunity to share our lives. Now, I would like to challenge you to host your own tea party and invite women to share their lives with you. Maybe we can start a tea party chain!"

"That's a great idea," Lynda said. "I'll have one."

"Me, too," Connie chimed in. Others nodded enthusiastically.

"I'm glad," I said with a chuckle. "And don't forget to invite me!"

Topics for Tea

If you decide to host your own Encourage Mint Tea Party, be sure to have a theme. At Connie's party, just before Valentine's Day, her guests shared how they had met their husbands. Tears were few and laughter was abundant. It was a wonderful way to discover a different side of people and to understand them on a deeper level.

Other topics you could incorporate into an Encourage Mint Tea Party might include the following:

- Tell a humorous moment from your life.
- Describe how you became a Christian.
- Talk about an adventure from your life.
- Tell a story from your childhood.

- ♥ Talk about a time God moved in your life.
- ♥ Tell a story about the birth of a child.
- ♥ Describe the craziest thing you ever did.
- ♥ Talk about a trial you have endured.
- ♥ Tell something no one knows about you.
- ♥ Share your most embarrassing moment.
- ♥ Tell a story about your children.
- ♥ Tell a romantic story, preferably about you.
- ♥ Describe the worst trouble you got into as a kid.
- ♥ Describe the best day of your life.
- ♥ Tell a story about a teenager in your life.
- ♥ Tell a story about a baby.
- ♥ Describe a time you were encouraged.
- ♥ Talk about your favorite book or movie. Give your reasons.
- ♥ Describe the craziest thing that ever happened to you at work.
- ♥ Talk about a time something nice happened to you.

Nurturing Moments

The time I spent with friends at my Encourage Mint Tea was special. How they inspired me! Women often miss out by not reaching out to one another. We must make the effort, whether it be a tea party, an exercise class, lunch with a friend, a Bible study or an accountability group.

Pam, an aqua-aerobics teacher, says, "My class is like an encouragement encounter. We exercise as we talk about our problems with our kids and jobs. We even had a surprise birthday party for one of our gals. She was thrilled when twenty of us showed up to wish her a happy fiftieth!"

Kim, wife of recording artist Steve Camp, is the mother of five children. She says, "I became involved in a group called The Young Mothers' Group. Three of us meet weekly with an older Christian woman for an hour and fifteen minutes. We share, study the Bible and pray for one another. It's been great to have someone I can talk to and to find support. It helps me put my priorities where they should be."

Christian recording artist and songwriter Mel Tunney founded her own group, FRIENDS, to help her stay accountable to other women. "When I share my temptations and choices," she says, "I benefit. I have someone who prays for me more intelligently and I have to learn to deal with what I've shared. It revitalizes my walk with the Lord and my personal life."

Finding an Encourager

Finding an encourager or someone to nourish you, can be a challenging task, but your efforts will pay off in great rewards. Mel Tunney says, "First, let God lead you to the right person. It may be someone you never dreamed would help. I prayed about who would be in the FRIENDS group and ended up calling a couple of people I felt close to, a couple of people I hadn't seen in a while and a few people I had always wanted to know."

If you don't have time to start an accountability group, look for a friend with whom you could occasionally share over lunch. Sharon, a pastor's wife, suggests you talk to others at your church and ask them to recommend a wise older woman who might be willing to nurture you. "Word of mouth may give you the best leads," Sharon says.

A few years ago, I started my own encouragement group. We met once a month for one year to pray for one another. I needed that prayer. The advice and support of my friends lifted me during difficult times. Although schedule conflicts now keep us from meeting, I still seek support and wisdom from those same women.

If you're not involved in sharing with a friend, perhaps you should prayerfully seek one. As women, we need to make an extra effort to be involved in each other's lives. It's a gift we not only need to take but need to give.

"It's worth the time and energy!" says Vickie Kraft.

Four

Encouraging News

Discouragement is all around us. We see it in the eyes of strangers, friends and family members. I saw it recently in the eyes of a young mother while my family and I were visiting Texas on the day before Thanksgiving. We arranged to stop in the town of Denton to visit an old college chum, now a professor at North Texas State University, his wife, Kay and their three kids.

“Would you like to come with me to the International Women’s Fellowship?” Kay asked me.

“Tell me about it,” I said.

“It’s a ministry sponsored by our church,” she explained. “We reach out to the wives of the international students who attend North Texas. Today they’re going to sample a Thanksgiving meal. I’m in charge of the English lesson.”

"Sounds great. I'd love to go!" I said.

I was delighted to meet young women from around the globe. The Thanksgiving story, along with the turkey, stuffing and pies, was met with giggles, oohs and aahs. Kay taught the English lesson masterfully. Later, another woman taught a simple Bible lesson. She asked us to share prayer requests with one another when we divided into groups.

A beautiful, chocolate-skinned mother from Ghana turned to me. Her large, brown eyes brimmed with worry. "Please pray for me," she said. "I'm very homesick. I just had my first baby and I'm overwhelmed trying to be wife, mother, cook and housekeeper. The custom in my country is for the grandmother to move into your home and care for the new baby. If I were back in Ghana, my mother would tend the baby while I concentrated on my home duties and my husband. I'm exhausted trying to do it all."

I wholeheartedly agreed to pray, but I couldn't help but stifle a smile as I silently thought, Welcome to America, the land where women are expected to do and be all things to all people at all times!

No wonder we sometimes get discouraged in the face of our responsibilities. At the top of those piles of laundry and dirty dishes, we also have to iron out difficulties with our kids, husband, jobs, coworkers and bosses. Sometimes it's hard to wash and wear these responsibilities without a sigh—or worse yet, angry words.

When Discouragement Crushes

While we are trying to smooth out difficulties, we are sometimes faced with scorching words of discouragement. Francie told me, "Once I planned and prepared a holiday dinner for my extended family. As an act of love, I painstakingly cleaned my small home, polished my silver, pulled out my best china and prepared the feast. I could hardly wait for the big event. I envisioned the meal to be a time of love and sharing. I imagined the gratitude my efforts would reap as my family thanked me for the special warmth and laughter."

Francie's dreams of gratitude were dashed, however, when her mother-in-law looked up from her slice of warm pumpkin pie and surveyed the table with a critical eye. She said, "Next year, I will do Thanksgiving at my house. There's not enough room here, your turkey was underdone and your stuffing was dry. Where did you find that recipe anyway?"

Francie was crushed. Her mother-in-law's words of criticism made her feel her efforts were not good enough. Later, Francie said, "For months afterward, I found it difficult to offer hospitality to Jeff's mom."

I remember one of the first times I faced hard words of criticism. I was on the yearbook staff in high school and had spent hours selecting photos and writing copy. When the books came out, I was pleased. After school, I went to the auditorium for play rehearsal. Gushing with pride, I asked a classmate how he liked the new yearbook.

Although I would never repeat his caustic, vulgar reply, I will say I was shocked, then infuriated. My happy, easygoing demeanor exploded as I threw my schoolbooks onto the floor and ran to the girls' bathroom. I hid in a stall, sobbing and I'd still be there if the drama coach hadn't sent in a couple of girls to coax me out. Humiliated, I had learned just how painful criticism could be, especially when it concerned my writing. Bruce's harsh words stung me deeply because they spelled rejection of something that was part of me.

Reject Rejection

Rejection is one of the hardest forms of discouragement to overcome. Darla complained, "My best friend disappeared when I miscarried for the fourth time. Because she was pregnant, I figured she withdrew because she thought it would be difficult for me to see her blossoming belly. Actually, it was not seeing her that was difficult."

Patsy, a widow, has also felt the sting of rejection. She said, "When a friend asked me what I'd be doing for Christmas, I said, 'I have no plans.' Then Donna asked a couple who was standing near me the same question. When the couple also answered, 'Nothing,' Donna turned her back on me and invited them to Christmas dinner. I spent the holiday alone."

Ridicule, intentional or unintentional, is another problem that brings severe discouragement. One woman relates, "When my children were young, I took ice-skating lessons with them. I decided to surprise my husband with my accomplishment. When he came to watch, he said to me, 'Is that as well as you can do, even after lessons?' I was crushed and never ventured onto the ice again."

It also hurts when someone does not believe in us or accuses us falsely. A retired secretary told me, "It seems petty now, but in high school I was in the National Honor Society one semester as a junior. I'd made straight As and a B and I was proud of this accomplishment. The next semester I got a C in biology because my teacher said I hadn't turned in one of my drawings. I had turned in the report and all my grades had been good, but her grade kept me out of the honor society. I was crushed, angry and embarrassed. I didn't forgive her for many years."

No wonder many of us get discouraged. I asked several women to rate areas where they needed encouragement. The number-one area was prayer support, followed by the need for a listening ear, then a hug, thanks for a job well done and finally, encouraging words. Other areas women rated as important were (in descending order) reassurance, sincere compliments, fresh ideas and sound advice.

Good News

The good news is encouragement bridges pitfalls so we can cross over to success. Verna describes how encouragement helped her overcome an obstacle in her life's path. She explains, "When I was nineteen, I graduated from business school, then went to work as a legal secretary. There was so much to learn, I became discouraged. My mother showed me I had two choices: quit the job or do my best to learn the job. I chose to do my best and worked in the field for twenty-seven years."

Not only is encouragement a gift that supports others, it also supports the one who gives the gift. Dorothy Weatherly told me how encouragement was instrumental in her quest to encourage others. "Since I serve on the Chinese council at First Baptist Church of Beaumont, Texas, I wanted to learn Mandarin," she says. "What challenge and frustration! I can speak only a little of this difficult language. But all of my Chinese friends encouraged me. Seeing the look of surprised pleasure on the face of a new friend when I speak in her language has made it worth the effort."

Author Dianne E. Butts is thankful for the support her friend Betty has given her. She writes, "Betty's encouragement comes often and in small doses, so it's hard to pinpoint specific examples. But that's OK, because it's more like I am a drinking glass, upside-down in the dishwasher and she's the water. None of the water remains in the glass. Through each splash of cleansing water, the glass is renewed, refreshed, made clean and prepared to be used again and again. Encouragement washes away any bitter residue that brings discouragement and then coaxes us toward usefulness again and again."

It Takes Time to Encourage

The hardest part of investing in someone is giving the gift of time, the most expensive resource we possess. But when we spend time on others, it comes back with interest. How many of us are willing to make this kind of investment? Caught up in the rush of life, we pass by the people God may have put in our paths.

I often hear women express loneliness. Katrina told me, "I wish my friends would spend time with me. But everyone's too busy."

Ann Marie said, "A quick phone call, cheery card or lunch invitation goes a long way in saying, 'I care.'"

Dianne E. Butts also expressed the importance of investing time when she wrote to tell me, "My husband and I had only been married about a year when we moved to Steamboat Springs, Colorado. I got a job right away and that's where I met Linda Dennison-Kemry. She seemed to take a special interest in me. I was in my early twenties, while she was about ten years older.

"Linda never seemed satisfied to sit back and just let friendships happen—she worked at them. She scheduled time for us to spend together once a month, even after we both moved on to different jobs. She always had something planned, not just to go out to do something but at home, too.

"Linda was famous for packing around grocery sacks full of 'stuff.' She'd show up at my house with several full sacks. Her passion was creating beautiful stained glass window hangings. One year she made Christmas presents for family members and allowed me to help her cut and solder pieces together. (Guess what I got for Christmas that year!)

She also taught me to crochet and quilt and even taught me how to brand calves! Linda gave me far more than she knew, gently encouraging me to believe in myself. Spending time with me, she taught me I was worthwhile, valuable and important. And as if that weren't enough, Linda gave me the greatest gift ever: she invited me to church and began a Bible study for just the two of us. She helped me know a God who believes I am worthwhile, valuable and important. Linda taught me by example to be an encourager and a godly mentor. Now I, too, strive to encourage other women to know God and live for him."

What an example of friendship and encouragement Linda sets for the rest of us. Not only did Linda reach out to Dianne, she mentored her and shared her faith. When Dianne moved to Eastern Colorado, I wonder who had the harder time saying good-bye, Dianne or Linda? The gift Linda imparted was priceless. Her influence will always remain in Dianne's life. The greatest accomplishment is that Dianne learned to reach out, to invest her life and time in others through the Lord.

The time we spend with someone else may seem unimportant. But we are always setting an example. We may never know how much this investment will increase.

I wanted to pass on this poem as a reminder of how valuable your investments can be, not only in friends but also in your children. As you reach out to friends, don't forget to reach back to your family.

You Are the Lesson

You are the life lesson—
Your children read each day.
They've seen the deeds you've done,
They've studied all your ways.
They watch all that you do,

They hear all that you say.
Someday they'll be like you,
So do your best today.

We must remember the value of encouragement and time invested in children. Deborah, a mother and homemaker, knows how valuable this can be. She told me when tragedy hit her family, a friend drove eight hundred miles just to be with her. Deborah knows her friend made a great sacrifice to perform this act of mercy.

This reminds me of a quote attributed to Carol Burnett: "I think we're here for each other."

So true! We are here to help and support one another.

The Thrill of Encouraging Others

The answer to the question of how to be encouraged is in encouraging others. To those who are lonely, why not try spending yourself on others. This is the way to turn loneliness into joyful relationships. There is nothing quite like the thrill of realizing you've made a difference in someone's life and that your words or actions have helped someone who is hurting. If you want to find encouragement, give it away.

Molly proved this point. She told me, "I was going through a difficult divorce due to my husband's ongoing infidelity. One of the hardest things I had to do was to call my best friend and break my secret.

"The next day, feeling down, I was both surprised and moved when my friend dropped by to see how I was doing. But the funny thing was, instead of talking about my impending divorce, we talked about her marriage. I ended up supporting her relationship with her husband. When she left, I knew she was encouraged. But I was on cloud nine. Later, I told God, 'This is so like you. Just when I am at the mouth of the pit, you send someone to me whom I can encourage. Thank you.'"

Encouragement Types

I have noticed people with different personality styles encourage others according to their own strengths and weaknesses. Our goal is to allow Christ to balance our weaknesses with his strengths. The Greek philosopher, Hippocrates, taught there are four basic behavioral patterns:

Sanguine: Outgoing, talkative, optimistic

Choleric: Goal-oriented, driven, achiever

Phlegmatic: Quiet, contemplative, dependable

Melancholic: Sensitive, detailed, perfectionist

Each of us is a unique combination of these personality styles. You may find you're both Sanguine and Choleric, with Choleric dominating. You may find yourself to be Melancholy and Phlegmatic. It's important to keep in mind there is no right or wrong combination. You're exactly the personality type God made you to be.

To help determine which of these styles is most like you, read the descriptions below, ranking them from one (most like you) to four (least like you). The top two categories will most likely reflect your dominant and secondary styles, although you may find you have some characteristics of the other temperaments as well. Note that many people who consider themselves to be all four groups are most likely Phlegmatic or Melancholic, because these types can see themselves in every style.

Clues from your personality style will show how you relate to and encourage others:

Sanguine

The chattiest of the four styles, she loves to encourage through an abundance of words. She's upbeat, friendly and likes to praise others. She's known for warm hugs and is often designated official "greeter" and "encourager."

The sanguine is the most likely temperament to use exhortation, encouraging words, and hugs. She's compassionate and is often moved to tears. She needs to realize that some personality styles are not as "touchy-feely" and may not enjoy her hugs as much as others.

Choleric

The choleric woman loves to give advice. God has placed in her the capacity to make sense out of situations and she often has the innate ability to know the right thing to do. She loves to teach and set things right. She's the least likely temperament to encourage through a hug. Words of praise don't often escape her lips.

The choleric has a hard time understanding that many of her friends may not want her advice and she's often frustrated when they refuse to follow it. She needs to learn to let go, allowing friends to make their own mistakes. She needs to let her friends know when she thinks they're doing a good job.

Phlegmatic

The phlegmatic woman is a loyal, gifted listener. She loves to soak in the words of her friends. Her insights are usually wise because she has spent much time observing life. She's willing to listen to advice but seldom applies it to her own life because she likes to do things her way. She's unobtrusive and you may have to work to get her to tell you what she thinks. But when she does, you'll be glad you listened.

She needs to work at verbally responding to her friends, making an effort to let them know when they are on the right track. Unless asked, she usually will not give her opinion. When she does tell what she's thinking, she worries about offending others. She works hard to walk the middle line.

Melancholic

The melancholic is the most sensitive of the four temperaments. She cares deeply about the feelings of others but may be hypersensitive. She's able to "read" people, taking cues from their words, body language, pauses and facial expressions. Being sensitive, she sometimes misreads these cues and thinks she's hurt someone's feelings. She apologizes for imagined wrongs.

The feelings of a melancholic are sometimes hurt by those with less sensitive temperaments who may never realize they have stepped on her toes. She needs to learn to forgive and let go of grudges. She's a caring friend who often pours herself into sacrificial acts of kindness.

In a survey to research the relationship of encouragement style to personality type, I was surprised to discover the effectiveness of encouragement seems to be related more to a person's emotional attitude than to personality type. A person with a driven personality may not be a natural hugger and may even cringe when hugged in greeting. But at the loss of a loved one, this same person may find healing in the arms of a warm hug.

A woman who would not normally talk out her problems may sometimes need to vent to a listening ear. A person who feels self-sufficient and does not believe in God will probably melt like putty when a friend prays with her during a personal tragedy. A person who often shirks advice may sometimes be willing to accept it and a person who loves to talk may pause long enough to hear needed words of comfort.

After our study of the four temperaments, the most important factor in determining the kind of encouragement to offer should be the factor of love. Any form of encouragement based on love will be effective, for love makes all the difference.

It Can Be Hard to Encourage

It can be hard to reach out to someone who is hurting. We want to help, not to make things worse. What do we do? What do we say? Have you tried to encourage someone and felt as if your words had the impact of a wilted pansy? Would you give yourself an A for effort but an F for effectiveness? Is avoiding the hurting person the answer? No, of course not, because avoidance will feel like rejection.

The secret behind any effort to encourage is to care enough to try. Be careful—do you want to encourage or manipulate? These are two separate agendas. Make sure your motives are pure. Then, even if your actions and words are all wrong, your friend will see your heart is right.

It Can Be Humbling to Hearten

Sometimes, the process of uplifting someone can be a humbling experience. Kathy Collard Miller shared this story with me: "Sitting in the airport, waiting for my flight to leave, I couldn't seem to concentrate on my book. I kept glancing at the snack counter, wondering whether I should get something to eat. Suddenly, I sensed the Lord whisper in my heart, 'Go tell the woman at the counter I love her.'

"'Oh, Lord, you know I don't like to do things like that,' I prayed. 'People always think I'm weird.'

"I could sense the Lord waiting patiently. After trying to think of any good reason to refuse, I gave in. As I stood in line, I was surprised when no one came up behind me to order. By the time I was at the counter, no one was around, except the fiftyish black woman behind the counter. 'May I help you?' she asked.

"'Yes, I'd like a glass of iced tea,' I said. Hesitating, I felt the Lord's firm nudge. 'But I also wanted to tell you that God loves you.'

"The woman's face registered shock. 'Oh no,' I thought. 'See what happens when you make me do this,

Lord? Now I've offended her.' But within seconds, her face softened and tears sprang to her eyes.

"The woman whispered through a choked throat, 'You don't know how much I needed to hear that. My husband died three months ago and I've been feeling like God didn't care. . . .' She couldn't continue but fixed my iced tea, followed me to get my sugar and poured out her grief. No one came up to the counter while we talked and I was able to encourage her. As we parted, she leaned over and hugged me.

"I walked away thinking, 'Lord, when I think you want to embarrass me, you take my reluctant obedience and use it for your glory. Thank you!'"

Kathy's story encouraged me to be more willing to follow those gentle nudges from God to reach out to others. I believe God has called us to hearten friends and family:

H Hugs
E Listening ears
A Advice
R Relief for grief
T Good turns
E Earnest prayer
N Nice words

In the following chapters, we'll take a look at ways to do just that!

Five

Hugs to Embrace

A wise man once said, "A hug is the perfect gift: one size fits all and no one minds if you exchange it."

But is this true?

Consider this: you're at your family reunion and here comes Aunt Sophia. Triple chins bounce against her ample bosom and jiggling arms are outstretched as she waddles toward you. All the while, she croons a love song, "Look at you, dear. I could just eat you up!"

You know what's next. You're about to be surrounded on every side. You brace yourself, surrendering. Aunt Sophia's fleshy arms wrap you in their warmth. You tense, relax, then it's over. She steps back, admiring you, then smiles with delight and says, "It's so good to see you."

Ahhh, you've just been hugged.

Hugging is an important element of encouragement. So why were you nervous? Maybe because hugs are intimate. I don't always enjoy hugs from folks outside my immediate family, unless I'm caught in the excitement of the moment. It's not that I don't care or that I'm a cold fish, it may be that I'm not ready to demonstrate my feelings. I need time to prepare emotionally for this sensitive dose of encouragement. OK, call me part choleric if you must. I do have a goal-oriented streak. This may be why I sometimes grimace when I see a hug coming my way. In the arms of a hugger, I may secretly twitch with discomfort, yet I'm glad to know I'm loved.

Hugs are a warm way to express love and caring, important parts of well-being. Research shows babies and those in elder care do not thrive emotionally, physically or mentally without regular hugs and human touch. Also, believe it or not, hugs are scriptural. The apostle Paul implored Christians to "greet one another with a holy kiss" (2 Cor 13:12). Can't you imagine the saints of long ago embracing and smooching? And that was before deodorant, toothpaste and breath mints!

As I study Scripture, I understand that Jesus hugged others. In accounts of his life, we read that the apostle John leaned against him at the Passover table (see Jn 13:23, KJV). This leaning was a hug-like gesture that men of today do not often practice. Perhaps if there were a 33 A.D. Jerusalem Manners Guide, it would tell you such manly displays of affection were socially acceptable at the time of Christ.

Jesus also hugged children brought to him by their mothers, much to the disgust of his disciples. Whenever he wasn't looking, the twelve men would try to shoo away the little visitors. "What?" they may have said. "You say you don't have an appointment? Too bad. The Master is busy now. Besides, he doesn't take unsolicited hugs."

Jesus reprimanded the twelve do-gooders for trying to protect him from pint-sized interruptions. He turned to the children, opened his arms and said, "Let the little children come to me . . ." (Mt 19:14). I can see him scooping the children into his lap for a hug and a blessing. How tender, sweet and intimate! In this way, Christ modeled encouragement and welcome in armloads of hugs.

The Importance of Personal Touch

What do hugs do? Avonne says, "A hug can convey warmth and concern in a way words can't. It communicates a willingness to get close."

I agree. Hugging is a daily part of my routine. In the years since my daughter's accident, I have enjoyed cuddling her in my arms. Although severely disabled, with a limited capacity for communication, Laura radiates joy during our hugging sessions. I love to snuggle with her even though she's able to return the embrace only with her heart—a heart filled with innocence and love. Dozens of daily hugs from her contain a power strong enough to bring tears to my eyes.

When asked why I radiate peace, I often say, "I get to hug Laura every day!" It is a privilege to be envied and it is interesting to note how much I, the hugger, get out of those cuddles with my daughter.

The act of hugging gives strength, not only to the huggee but to the hugger. Recently, I discussed the art of hugging with a psychotherapist friend. She told me hugs contribute significantly to a person's recovery process. She related a story about a depressed patient transferred to her care after a previous psychotherapist had given up. "'Glenda' will never recover," she was told. The patient was at the point of suicide.

"Glenda was not able to hug others," Dr. Clare explained. "She shied away from physical touch."

Week after week, Dr. Clare encouraged Glenda to reach out and finally, to embrace others. Now, this young woman has discovered the joy of hugging. No longer is Glenda suicidal. She's more content and is able to face her problems from a position of strength.

"Glenda found her breakthrough when she found her ability to hug," says Dr. Clare.

Hugs Are Popular with Everyone

When my sister-in-law, Mary, taught second grade to a group of underprivileged children, she always ended the day with "H&H"—handshake or hug. She would stand at the door to her room and let the children say good-bye by picking which they wanted.

Mary reports: "The children usually picked a hug, except for a few shyer boys who always picked a handshake. I think these hugs and handshakes were important because many of the children were not hugged at home. They needed the warm human contact saying, I love you and I care."

Hugs That Made a Difference

Karen told me, "When my mom died of cancer a few years ago, hugs and physical closeness of friends and family gave me more comfort and strength than words."

I will never forget one ill-gained hug that helped me during the months following the car accident that handicapped our Laura. I struggled with overwhelming grief and wanted our old life back; the life where I was busy reading my little girl's favorite books as she cuddled in my lap, playing peekaboo, discovering the joys of dripping ice cream cones, puppies and backyard sand castles. Our normal life seemed gone forever as Laura remained in a coma.

The day came when Laura was released from the hospital. She came home with a life support machine, feeding tubes, oxygen and an army of care-givers who sat in my kitchen monitoring her (and my) every move. At night, I cried myself to sleep for my lost daughter and because our loving home had been turned into a sterile hospital ward. It seemed there was no place I could escape the watchful eyes of pity.

How I longed to appear normal to friends and strangers, but even quick trips to the grocery store brought tears to my eyes as I watched other mothers with children. Once a clerk asked me why I was buying so many diapers, expecting me to joyfully tell her about all my little ones. I stared at her, trying to find words to describe how my beautiful toddler was now paralyzed, blind, mute, unconscious and incontinent. The words would not come as I froze before her, valiantly trying to choke back tears. Her smile stiffened as I finally stammered, "They're for my handicapped daughter."

Going to church brought no relief. Everyone was full of loving concern, but I was tired of that. I wanted to talk about normal things. I wanted to laugh. I wanted to be normal again. One Sunday morning, when my husband was out of town, I decided to drive to church in a neighboring town where no one knew me. They will think I'm normal, I reasoned. They will not be able to see my broken heart.

I spent a lot of time selecting bright clothes and primping in front of the mirror. I grabbed my earrings, dashed to the van and headed for the freeway. I rushed into the sanctuary and found a seat. My presence seemed to evoke bright eyes and wide smiles from my fellow worshipers. Ah, I thought, they're accepting me at face value. They see me as a regular person!

During the sermon, I noticed the preacher kept looking in my direction as he summarized his thoughts on the silliness of some Christians. I tried to look wise, nodding deeply at every point. After the service, the woman in front of me turned to welcome me. A strange look swept across her face. Suddenly, she threw her arms around me and gathered me into a huge hug, a hug I gladly accepted.

Still, I couldn't help but think I had somehow blown my cover. She knows something is wrong. But how? A few minutes later, when I peeked in the church's bathroom mirror, I realized that somehow in my mad rush, I had grabbed mismatched earrings! I wore one large, gold-rimmed, red earring on my right ear and a huge, rainbow-colored, rhinestone-studded earring on my left ear. My Dumbo-sized mistake had blown my cover!

I glowed with embarrassment all the way home, imagining how I must have looked to the pastor as I encouraged his message on silly Christians with my smiles and nods. Yet, I was glad to find compassion in the arms of the woman who hugged me. Her physical touch of love was so healing to my tired and heavy heart. It was exactly what I needed to feel normal once again. That hug helped me through the months leading to my daughter's emergence from her coma. Most of us don't realize how important a hug can be to someone who is hurting.

My mother discovered the power of hugs one terrifying day. My nineteen-year-old brother, Jimmy, was riding in the backseat of a van with several fraternity brothers. At 2:00 a.m. a drunk driver swerved toward them on a divided highway and veered into their path with an impact that knocked off one of the van's front wheels which caused it to flip end over end.

Miraculously, four of the boys escaped serious injury, but Jimmy lay on the side of the road, unconscious and still. A man on an oil derrick station witnessed the accident and called for an ambulance.

Later, my parents were told by the hospital staff, "Your son is at the point of death. He probably won't be alive when you get here."

They rushed to the hospital and when they arrived, Jimmy was still alive, although he had a concussion, a crushed arm, a cracked kidney, a shattered vertebra and other internal injuries. "The next morning, as we sat in the ICU waiting room," Mom says, "Jimmy's fraternity brothers arrived to wait with us. One by one, these boys wrapped me in their arms. The accident happened over a decade ago, but I still get goose bumps when I think about those hugs; I can still feel them. There is power in a hug!"

That power helped my mother through the next few days, weeks, then months. Thankfully, Jimmy did survive and against all odds, learned to walk again. A few years later, we had the privilege of seeing him walk down the aisle with his beautiful bride. Today he has a family of his own.

As my mom looks back, she realizes she was given the gift of hope for Jimmy in the arms of his friends.

When to Hug

As we've seen, arms that give hugs gather love. Still, it's important to be sensitive about when to hug and when not to hug. For example, I never miss an opportunity to wrap my arms around my children or my husband, while a cheek-to-cheek hug works well with my friends. When a standoffish friend or an opposite-sex friend not related by birth or marriage needs a hug, I avoid the full-body hug and offer a pat-on-the-back or a side-to-side hug, which seem less intimidating and intimate but still offers encouragement.

Yes, there is a time to hug and a kind of hug for every occasion. There is also a time not to hug. Ecclesiastes 3:1-5 says:

> There is a time for everything, and a season for every activity under heaven: a time to be born and a time to die, a time to plant and a time to uproot, a time to kill and a time to heal, a time to tear down and a time to build, a time to weep and a time to laugh, a time to mourn and a time to dance, a time to scatter stones and a time to gather them, a time to embrace and a time to refrain.

It's best to watch the changing moods of the seasons to discern how and when to hug. These include times we want to say:

"I love you": One of my favorite reasons to hug my husband and children! The hugs keep them grounded in my affection.

"Thank you": Roberta wrote, "Every morning I get a hug and a thank you from my kids." (I'm thinking, Wow, what neat kids; do you reckon she ever loans them out?)

"I care": The apostle Paul gave a CPR-like hug, saving the life of a young man who fell asleep and fell to his death from a third-story window while Paul was preaching (see Acts 20:10).

"Congratulations": Watch the hugs at the next graduation ceremony you attend; they'll be all around you!

"Welcome": Welcome hugs mean "It's good to see you," and "I'm glad you're here."

"I missed you": These hugs convey emotion when words fail. In Luke 15, Jesus tells about a boy who decided he was allergic to hauling hay around the family farm and demanded his inheritance. Setting off for fun and fame, he blew his entire stash of cash on good times and fast friends. Eventually, penniless and shamed, he headed home, fearing his father's response. But at the gates of the farm, his father dropped everything, ran and threw his arms around the boy. What a hug!

"I'm sorry": Some hugs happen after confrontations. My favorite is when my son was five and climbed into my lap, wrapping his arms around my neck to lisp, "I won't paint the mirror with your lipstick again." Another version of this hug is the one that communicates, "I'm grieving with you." When I was hysterical with grief when my husband was temporarily lost in the mountains, a friend came over. She didn't lecture or comment; she simply hugged.

"God loves you": Billy Graham tells of meeting Mother Teresa and how the night before she'd held five dying people in her arms. When he asked why she did what she did, she quietly pointed to the figure of Christ on the cross hanging on her wall.[1]

God Hugs Us

One of the most exciting things about hugs is knowing that God hugs us. Psalm 139:7-10 says:

> Where can I go from your Spirit? Where can I flee from your presence? If I go up to the heavens, you are there; if I make my bed in the depths, you are there. If I rise on the wings of the dawn, if I settle on the far side of the sea, even there your hand will guide me, your right hand will hold me fast.

Not only does God hold onto us, we can hold onto him. The apostle Paul writes:

> I want to know Christ and the power of his resurrection and the fellowship of sharing in his sufferings, becoming like him in his death, and so, somehow, to attain to the resurrection from the dead. "Not that I have already obtained all this, or have already been made perfect, but I press on to take hold of that for which Christ Jesus took hold of me" (Philippians 3:10-12).

The next time you're feeling discouraged, remember who is hugging you. It is the God of the universe. His love for you will never fail, for he's holding on tight.

Six

Ears to Hear

One of the least expensive, yet more valuable gifts we can give to friends and family is a hearing ear. The price you pay to listen to someone is only your time, emotional energy and empathy. Unfortunately, there are not many people willing to spend their time on this gift. We would rather be listened to than listen. James reminds us: “Take note of this: Everyone should be quick to listen, slow to speak and slow to become angry” (Jas 1:19). What would happen if we really practiced this teaching? Not only would it revolutionize our circle of influence, it would revolutionize the world.

Usually, only our dear phlegmatic sisters practice this art effectively. Still, I have to wonder: When Ms. Phlelina Phlegmatic is nursing her cup of warm tea at my kitchen table, is she quiet because she’s listening to what

I'm saying or is she silently trying to decide what to cook for dinner? No one will ever know, but listening is a skill that, regardless of personality type, can be developed to a higher level. When used properly, it will encourage others.

The Importance of Listening

I needed a listener when my daughter spent a year in a coma. I didn't want to further burden my family with my pain; they were struggling with their own. I couldn't go to my friends, because many of them simply could not handle my crisis and our church was between pastors. I ended up feeling like a volcano with no relief valve, ready to explode. How could I vent unless I had someone to talk to?

In frustration, I made an appointment with a Christian counselor. I paid this dear man many bucks an hour just so I could talk—as fast as I could, until he interrupted me to tell me our time was up. My words poured forth at breakneck speed, faster and faster, as I raced the clock. I found comfort in vocalizing my thoughts and experiences. It was wonderful to have a listener who attended my words so patiently, with nods, comments and prayers. I would go home feeling emotionally exhausted, but spiritually renewed.

Do Christians need a counseling license to be good listeners? I think not. Nancy told me she spent several days at a family gathering listening to Robert talk about his wife who had died a year earlier of cancer.

At last Robert apologized. "Nancy, I'm sorry," he said. "I didn't mean to go on like this."

Nancy gave him a hug and patted his back. "It's OK," she said. "Talking is healing."

Robert smiled, "You're so wise."

He's right. Nancy was wise to let Robert grieve verbally. It was a beautiful gift.

Permission to talk is a gift often given at Jewish funerals. A whole day is set aside to remember the dearly departed. Stories and memories are shared between tears, tissues and smiles. How bonding that experience must be for those left behind. What a blessing it must be for the friends and family of the deceased.

The sad thing is that most people are not allowed to talk about their departed friends and family. Anne Rosberger, executive director of the Bereavement and Loss Center in New York City, says: "It takes a lot of talking and most people get tired of listening. They want you to move on."[1]

How much time should bereavement take? Author Glen Davidson says most people in one survey felt recovery from a major loss should be accomplished in two weeks.[2] Christian counselor H. Norman Wright says, however, "The average grief-recovery time from an accident is averaged at three years, a suicide in the family is four years and homicide is five. If the loss is that of your own child, recovery may never be fully achieved."[3]

Who has the patience to give this kind of intensive attention? Most people don't. Lending an ear is an expense of both emotion and time. After all, it hurts to hear your friend's pain. Is it worth the investment? Well, unless your listening relationship is affecting your own emotional health or allowing your friend to be codependent upon you, the answer is yes! Your gift is worth more than a hundred bucks an hour as it will help your friend rise above despair, plus it will deepen your friendship. How can you put a price on that?

As you spend your time listening, don't expect too much too soon. Your heartbroken friend may not be able to shape up overnight. In fact, the listening process could take weeks, months or even years. But your listening ear could make all the difference.

When Listening Makes a Difference

Many people have written to tell me about times they have ministered to others through the gift of listening. Carla just sat quietly with a neighbor who had lost her twenty-year-old son in an out-of-state accident. I can imagine the scene. The phone rings and Carla picks it up. She hears the shocking news and tells her friend, "I'll be right over."

Quickly, Carla grabs her purse and heads for the door. Minutes later, she's sitting with her arm around Sandy. Can't you picture Sandy sitting at her kitchen table? Perhaps the birds are singing, but she can't hear them. She wants to scream, but she's frozen in shock. All she can do is sit in silence. But Carla is there. Sandy can feel Carla's embrace. She feels comforted in the silence.

Another woman told me about the difference listeners had made in her life. "I will always be in debt to two of my friends who spent time listening to me the year my life fell apart. My mom died, I moved to a new city, had financial difficulties and was confined to bed in order to rest during my pregnancy. I was an emotional wreck. Charla and Nicki came to my rescue. They spent hours sitting beside my bed as I poured out my heart. They made a commitment to listen. They were instrumental in helping me recover."

How to Listen

The hardest part of listening is learning to shut our own mouths. I have created a recipe to help my readers do just that:

Recipe for a Listening Ear

Cook's Note: Some friends give you their full attention without hearing a word you say. Don't make this mistake. Listening is a lasting gift. Give to everyone.

Ingredients:

1 friend
2 ears
1 mouth
1 banana
sprinkles of nods
loads of "hmmms" or grunts of acknowledgment
2 wide eyes

Directions:

To use your ears, you must shut your mouth. If your mouth won't shut, insert a ripe banana. Chew banana slowly or not at all. This will give your ears a chance to hear something other than the sound of your own voice.

As you listen, sprinkle your friend with nods, adding "hmmms" at will. If you are not nodding or hmming, your friend may feel compelled to repeat herself. If this should happen, widen your eyes and add occasional grunts of acknowledgment. Even if you never say a word, your friend may feel you are the greatest conversationalist in the world.[4]

Even advice well given does not contribute more encouragement than listening. Therefore, it's important to learn how to use this skill effectively. Friend and fellow author LeAnn Thieman, who wrote This Must Be My Brother, taught me a wonderful lesson on listening. LeAnn and I were driving to a meeting together when she said, "When my kids were younger, I took pride in the fact I was a good mother. One day, one of my friends asked me, 'Do you listen to your children?'

"'Of course I do,' I replied. 'I spend hours listening to my children.'

"'But do you really hear what they are saying?'

"'Absolutely!'

"Then my friend asked, 'But do you look into their faces when they talk?'

"I gulped. 'No, not always.'"

LeAnn gripped the steering wheel more tightly. "In fact, I spent little time making eye contact with my kids," she continued. "When my children came to me at the end of the day, I bustled around the kitchen while they talked. I was too busy peeling potatoes to look into their faces. When I realized this omission, I worried, My children are my priority and they may not even know it because I don't take the time to really look at them.

That day, LeAnn made a change. When her kids wanted to talk to her, she began to stop what she was doing and sit down with them at the table. She often had a cup of tea while her children told her about their day at school.

Seeing what the gift of attention meant to her children, LeAnn wondered, Perhaps I need to give my husband the same consideration.

And she did. She began to give her husband the gift of undivided attention when he spoke with her. Soon she realized she needed to expand this gift to her friends.

LeAnn looked at me out of the corner of her eye and said, "As a matter of fact, it's hard to drive this car and keep my eyes on the road. I really want to look into your eyes as we talk. But there's a time and a place for that."

I can vouch for LeAnn. When we have lunch together, she searches my eyes, paying careful attention to what I'm saying. LeAnn is an expert listener and her listening skills show she cares.

The Listener's Response

There are many responses a listener can offer to encourage a friend.

They include:

- Advice
- Patience
- Prayer
- Trust to keep the confidence
- Action
- Helpful questions
- Silence

Advice

Often we respond to a friend who shares an intimate need by giving advice. But advice is not always the proper response. Avonne reminded me, "I'm usually looking for someone to let me verbalize my thoughts so I can come to my own resolution. I'm not often looking for advice."

We will talk more about the advice response in a later chapter, but it is important to note that many people simply want to talk out a problem. If we give advice that's unwelcome or unneeded, it will often go unheeded anyway.

Patience

Recently, I was speaking on encouragement at a country club in Greeley, Colorado. During a discussion group, a woman I'll call Janie said, "I've suffered from illness for many years. It means so much that my friends have been faithful, maintaining a listening and loving relationship. They aren't looking for a friend they can fix. They're looking for a friend they can love. They don't just throw advice at me, then move on to their next project; they remain steady and patient, continuing to listen, despite my ongoing struggles."

Prayer

Prayer should be a natural response to a shared need. I will never forget how much my counselor's prayers meant to me when I was caught in the grief cycle. I think this is because when we are going through hard times, it's easy to forget God cares and hears our prayers. It feels good to know someone else is approaching God on our behalf. This kind of prayer gift goes a long way in helping us realize we are not forgotten.

Gaylene told me that when she started college, her roommate, Cyndi, encouraged her as she adjusted to being away from home for the first time. She says, "Cyndi talked things through with me, listened and prayed with me every evening."

Trust to Keep the Confidence

When someone shares a need or problem, it does not give us the freedom to share that need with others—even a prayer chain. The most important gift we can give may be to keep the confidence. Ask permission before you tell and ask permission before you call the prayer chain, because although a fabulous ministry, a prayer chain can unintentionally turn into a gossip mill.

Another recipe I'd like to share with you is called

How to Keep a Secret

Cook's Note: Keeping a secret does not mean lowering your voice when you tell it. Neither does it mean refusing to say who told it to you. To keep a secret means to not tell.

Ingredients:
Cup of unspilled beans, dash of forgetfulness

Directions:
Most people feel that secrets are a burden; they are eager to share them because it is nice to have someone else to help carry them. The problem arises because this process usually continues one person at a time, until the secret is public knowledge.

Use caution in sharing a secret of your own. After all, if you cannot contain it, why do you think your friends can?[5]

Action

Another appropriate listening response may be to take action. My friend Linda B recently went back to college to become an RN. She tells a hair-raising story about how she became an advocate for a patient: "During my first rotation," she says, "a homeless man came to the hospital with gangrene from frostbite. He had all ten toes removed. When he woke up from surgery, he was angry and yelled at the senior resident in charge of his case. In retaliation, the resident discontinued the man's pain medications.

"This man was my patient, too," Linda said. "I listened to his torment and finally got someone to reverse the resident's decision. The man died later, but his death was not filled with needless suffering. Because I took action, hospital policies were changed to prevent this kind of abuse from reoccurring."

Helpful Questions

Questions can prompt friends to discover truth for themselves, when they might reject the same truth if given as advice. We discuss this technique further in the next chapter, but you can help your friend by asking things like, "How do you feel about that?" and "How can you best resolve that?" These questions not only help your friend get a better grip on the situation, they also put her in touch with her emotions and help her think through the possible solutions.

Silence

If you don't know what to say, remember that may be God's way of telling you to listen. Whitney shared how she once came to this conclusion. She relates, "A friend called, in tears, to tell me her sister had died in Italy. She deeply grieved her sister's passing because she did not know if her sister was a believer. I prayed for wisdom as I drove to her house. What should I say? God answered my prayer: I said nothing; I listened."

When to Refrain From Listening

What do you do when your life is interrupted by a compulsive talker? There may be times when it would be wise to refrain from listening.

Lynette Pickering says, "Being a good listener does not mean you have to be a doormat. I had to learn that the hard way. My kids play soccer and one of the other soccer-moms began to call me every day. At first I enjoyed hearing from this woman, but soon her hour-and-a-half conversations began to wear. Lisa would call and talk nonstop, hardly pausing to breathe. I didn't know what to do, so I listened.

"After three years, I knew I had to make a change. I prayed about it and felt the Lord had put Lisa in my life for a reason. That's when I began to ask questions. I discovered Lisa had not received much support as a little girl and now she did not receive support from her husband. I began to understand her deep insecurities and was better able to tolerate the calls. Still, I needed relief from her long-winded, one-sided conversations.

"One day, I found courage to interrupt Lisa. 'Would you say we're friends?' I asked.

"'Of course we're friends,' she said. 'We love to talk on the phone.'

"'Lisa, when people ask me, do you think I tell them you're my friend?'

"'Of course.'

"'No, Lisa, I tell them I'm your friend. I do not tell them you're my friend.'

"'Why not?'

"'Well, what do you really know about me, my children or my husband?'

"'I've been meaning to ask you about yourself, but I never have,' Lisa admitted.

"'Then perhaps I'm not your friend but your counselor,' I said. 'If you were my friend, you would know something about me.'"

Lynette explained, "Having this conversation with Lisa was the best thing I could have done. Lisa still calls, but she has agreed not to chatter so much. Now she's more courteous and is learning to take an interest in me. I feel our relationship is finally taking a new direction; we're beginning to be friends."

There is discipline in the gift of listening: to refrain from our own need to chatter and to make eye contact whenever possible. Finally, we have to be able to choose the listening response that will most encourage our friend—advice, patience, prayer, trust to keep the confidence, action, helpful questions or silence.

On top of this, we must be willing to keep our friendships in balance. Although we want to encourage through listening, we don't want our friends to depend on us more than they do on God. If this should start to happen, we must lovingly guide our friends to release their dependency on us.

But keep in mind that just because a friend is in need of emotional support does not automatically mean she's codependent. Her dependency may be the temporary result of an emotional crisis, not an ongoing need to be controlled or manipulated. Only you, with God's help, can discern if your relationship has become unbalanced. If you find it has, react with as much love and compassion as you can to turn your dependent friendship into a healthy relationship.

You can do this by asking a series of questions much like those Lynette asked, instead of automatically giving advice. Ask, "What do you think you should do?" or "What does the Bible say about that? Have you prayed about this yet?" In this way, you gently take the focus off yourself and turn it onto your friend's ability to make decisions based on God's counsel through prayer and Bible study.

If your friend resists gentle nudgings, be direct. You could say, "Molly, I think that's between you and your husband," or "I'm not prepared to give my opinion about that. Why don't you ask your counselor or pastor and take it to the Lord?" Suggest a good book that might help her sort out her options and ask her to share her decision with you later.

If your friend continues to want listening support, you might interrupt, saying, "I wish I had more time to help you, but my family needs me right now. I'll call you when I can." Wait a few days and when you call back, start the conversation by telling her you have only twenty minutes to talk. At the end of that time, politely break in: "I'm out of time. I'll call you later." Repeat this process until she accepts she can't monopolize you or rely on you to make her decisions for her.

If you consistently give a codependent friend this kind of help, she will find she can no longer depend on you to work out her problems or be her counselor. You may encourage her to personal and spiritual growth. After all, that's what she needs most.

Listening Goals

Remember, the person talking reaps encouragement when you listen to her and you reap the joy of sharing patience and compassion. Besides, as American humorist Wilson Mizner once said, “A good listener is not only popular everywhere, but after a while he knows something.”

In times of crisis or pain, there is nothing as supportive as a listening friend. Our goal should be not only to be supportive without facilitating codependency but also to point our friend to God’s best. When we do this, we are God’s champions to those who hurt. That’s the best kind of listener to be!

Seven

Advice Speaks

Not everyone appreciates advice. Oh, many love to give it; it's just most don't want to take it—even when it's free. But advice can encourage when planted in love and it makes a tremendous impact on those willing to receive it.

Dr. Richard C. Halverson, former chaplain of the United States Senate, said, "You can offer your ideas to others as bullets or as seeds. You can shoot them, or sow them; hit people in the head with them, or plant them in their hearts. Ideas used as bullets will kill inspiration and neutralize motivation. Used as seeds, they take root, grow, and become reality in the life in which they are planted."[1]

I love this picture because it shows the positive power of advice sown in love and the destructive power of advice sown in judgment. It's amazing what God can do with advice sown in love. The apostle Paul said, "I planted the seed, Apollos watered it, but God made it grow" (1 Cor 3:6). Although this refers to the telling of the Good News, it can be applied to the sharing of good advice. God can take our good advice, sown lovingly in the good soil of a willing soul and make it blossom.

Many blossoms and fruit can grow from the seeds of good advice. In fact, nothing feels better than giving advice that can make a difference. For example:

> When you Inspire – She'll want to do it!
> When you Encourage - She knows she can do it!
> When you Inform - She understands how to do it!
> When you Motivate – She'll do it now!
> When you Transform – She's done it!

When Advice Helps

Good advice, well received, can be life-transforming. My friend Evelyn would testify to that. Evelyn told me about the time she advised her friend Helen on marriage. Helen's husband, Ted, had cheated on her and she had decided to get a divorce because she didn't know what else to do.

Evelyn told me, "Although I couldn't impose my own standards on Helen, we spent hours talking. I encouraged her to look for a creative way to respond. Eventually, Helen had her lawyer draw up a contract outlining the consequences of any future affairs by her husband. Ted signed it. They are still together, beginning to work things out."

Evelyn's advice helped save a marriage. Helen received a wonderful gift when she decided to listen to Evelyn and how rewarded Evelyn must feel!

Several years back, I got the rare opportunity to advise my own mother. She'd watched several confrontations between me and my adorable son, Jimmy, who had a rather strong will in those days. Mom secretly wondered why I didn't handle him as effectively as she felt she'd handled me when I was a child. Although she never said so, I knew she thought she could do a better job, that is, until she finally got the chance she'd been waiting for. A few days after eight-year-old Jimmy flew to Texas to spend a week with her she called me. "How do I get him to obey me?" she asked, trying to hide the exasperation in her voice.

I advised, "Be firm, Mom. When you say 'No,' mean it. And follow it up with 'No TV' unless he complies."

A few days later, Mom cheerfully reported, "Your advice worked! We're getting along much better now."

Happily, grandmother and grandson had no further interruptions to their weeklong fun.

Lynne Beaulieu wrote a story about a time her advice helped a coworker. "At my first job, the group of women I worked with varied in size, shape and temperament," she said. "But they had one thing in common—the desire to be accepted by one another. All were welcomed into the group; that is, all except Marlo.

"There appeared to be no redeeming qualities in Marlo," Lynne continued. "She was plain and physically awkward. Her manner of dress accentuated her poorest physical assets, while her sour disposition kept her isolated. I felt sorry for Marlo. She held us at arm's length, but I could see she wanted acceptance.

"One day Marlo told me she was having an anniversary date with her husband and wanted to look especially nice. I offered to help her get ready. I wondered if my abilities could meet her expectations. When I told our coworkers about Marlo's big date, they wanted to help too. Shyly, she accepted our ministrations. She listened, carefully considering our advice about makeup and hairstyle.

"Marlo was pleased with the results. The delight she radiated applied a style and grace to her countenance that couldn't come from a tube or brush. But her greatest joy came from knowing we had accepted her."

We Can't Heal Their Pain

Of course, there are times when advice won't help. For example, advice can't mend a broken heart. That kind of healing can only be accomplished through God and his time, a lesson I tried to explain to my friend Terri. One day she asked me, "Would you pray for me? I have several friends who are going through divorces. I think I'm failing them."

"How so?"

"Their husbands have left them. They've come to me for help but my advice doesn't seem to be working."

"You mean they're hurting and you feel responsible?"

"Exactly," Terri said.

"Let me ask, if one of your friends were robbed and shot and she came to you all battered and bandaged, would you feel responsible for what had happened to her?" I asked.

"Of course not."

"What is the best thing you could do for your friend at that point?"

"I guess, just be there, listen to her talk about it, let her know I love her and that I'm praying for her. But my husband has different expectations in this area," Terri explained.

"What do you mean?" I asked.

"He's gone to several men who were thinking about divorcing or having affairs and he told them they were wrong. Several have recommitted to their marriages."

"Think about it," I said. "What your husband did was biblical. He advised the aggressor. The aggressor has the power to change his course. But your friends were victims of circumstance. They arrived bruised and bleeding. You can't change what happened."

"But nothing I say seems to help."

"That's frustrating. There is nothing you can do to fix their pain. All you can really do is offer good advice, listen, pray and be there."

I can understand Terri's struggle. Her friends are hurting. But it's not Terri's responsibility to fix them. That would be impossible for although our words can comfort and advise, they can't heal. Besides, hurting people are looking for our understanding, not our explanations.

When to Give Advice

It's OK to give advice:

1. When a friend asks for it.
2. When you feel you have earned your friend's confidence.
3. When you're willing to risk the friendship in order to warn or counsel.
4. When you're willing to allow your friend to follow or ignore your advice.

The last two points are the most important. If you're ready to accept these conditions, then you're ready to offer advice. But be careful; advice can hurt both the giver and the receiver. You'll get your best results if you observe the following guidelines.

How to Give Advice

Speak in love. Before you open your mouth to speak, you must judge your heart and be certain you're speaking in the spirit of love, not the spirit of anger, criticism, jealousy, revenge or manipulation. Advice given in the wrong spirit can be harmful instead of helpful and can wound instead of heal. If your friend cannot trust your heart, she'll not be able to trust your words. Besides, the point may not be whether or not she takes your advice but that she knows you love and support her regardless.

Another reason why you must advise with love is because a person who is hurting may be carrying a lot of guilt. If you're not careful, instead of helping, you may only heap more condemnation on her head.

Also, advice given with love will help us refrain from arguments. Paul reminded Timothy:

"Don't have anything to do with foolish and stupid arguments because you know they produce quarrels. And the Lord's servant must not quarrel; instead, he must be kind to everyone, able to teach, not resentful. Those who oppose him he must gently instruct, in the hope that God will grant them repentance leading them to a knowledge of the truth, and that they will come to their senses and escape from the trap of the devil, who has taken them captive to do his will" (2 Timothy 2:23-26).

Accept your friend unconditionally. Be careful how you judge others and try to see them through God's eyes. Freda learned this one day when she was shopping at the mall with her four-year-old grandson, Jeremy. They happened upon a young woman who was covered with tattoos, wore multiple nose and lip rings and whose hair was dyed every color of the rainbow. To Freda's shock, Jeremy ran up to her and said, "You are so pretty!"

Freda said, "I imagine that was the first time this young woman had heard those words. It made me realize I needed to start looking at other people through the eyes of a child with a pure heart."

Be vulnerable. We want to advise, but we want to do it from a position of strength. Too often, we don't want to share our own struggles because we assume it will make us look weak. In reality, our friends listen better when we admit our personal battles. Late one night, I was online in a Christian chat room when I discovered a distraught teenager.

"I've been terribly abused," she typed across the screen, "but I have a way out. I have a gun. I'm planning to use it on myself to escape my pain."

I typed: "WAIT! Cindy, don't hurt yourself. God loves you."

She replied, "That's easy for you to say. You have your act together. I'm not like you."

"I have my struggles too," I replied. "But God is faithful."

"What do you struggle with?" she asked.

Thinking of my handicapped daughter, I simply typed: "Grief and loss."

I continued, "But through my grief and loss, God has been with me. He has been my comforter. He can be that for you, too. Cindy, please don't hurt yourself. Please find counseling."

After twenty minutes of encouragement, Cindy agreed to get help. A month later, she sent me an e-mail. "Thanks for intervening when you did," she wrote. "I was ready to end it all. But you encouraged me. I'm in counseling now and I'm feeling much better. Thank you."

I believe Cindy wouldn't have listened to me if I hadn't been vulnerable. It wasn't until she learned I also struggled that I won the right to give her advice.

Don't preach. No one wants a lecture. Use stories to get your point across. Instead of delivering a rebuke, tell your friend about a similar situation: "I remember a friend who had the same problem." This way you can share your message without wagging a finger in her face.

Ask questions. This is one of the most effective counseling techniques ever. The goal is to get your friend to advise herself. Instead of saying, "Don't get an abortion," say, "So you're pregnant. What are your options?"

Your friend might say, "I could have the baby or I could abort it."

Then say, "What would the consequences be of aborting your baby?"

Your friend might say, "I would escape the situation I'm in."

You could then say, "But how do you think you would feel about the abortion?"

Your friend might eventually admit, "I could never forgive myself."

Then you could get her to think this through by asking, "Is that what you want? What would be the worst thing that would happen if you had the baby?"

"I could be a single mom or I could give the baby up for adoption."

You get the point. Continue to probe your friend to work out possible scenarios and consequences. Before you know it, you will find your friend offering herself sound advice. It may be the same advice you would have given her, but with human nature being what it is, she's more likely to take this advice from herself than from you.

Pray. Whether your friend takes your advice or not, continue to pray she'll find wisdom and strength.

We Can't Make People Take Our Advice

The other morning I was in the beauty shop, getting my hair trimmed when a woman in a nearby chair said, "I asked my twelve-year-old granddaughter what she's been up to. She said, 'Fighting with my sister. We fought over our room all day yesterday, all night and all day today. My mom said we had to work it out. I tried. I told my sister what to do, but she wouldn't do it!'"

I couldn't help but laugh. How much easier it would be for each of us if friends, coworkers and family would only agree to do what we say!

I was leading a discussion group at a retreat when Paula, a middle-aged woman, spoke up, frustration edging her voice. "What should you do if someone always comes to you for advice, but never takes your advice or tries to fix what's wrong?" She sighed and shook her head. "I have a friend like that and I feel like I'm hitting my head against the wall."

Doris nodded. "I finally told a friend of mine that I would still be her friend but wouldn't discuss her problems with her anymore."

Paula asked, "Has this helped?"

"I'm not sure," Doris admitted. "She's not speaking to me!"

Janet added, "One of my favorite sayings is 'You can't want more for somebody than they want for themselves.' But this is a tough balance, like with our teens and grown-up kids. We want so much for them, but we have to let them make their own decisions. Besides, when it comes to a problem like a friend with cancer, we can't fix it. All we can do is point them to God."

It's not up to you to force someone to take the right path. You can only present options.

If you've ever driven down a freeway through a sunny California orange grove, you may have had an experience like mine. It was a beautiful day and I was enjoying the aroma of blossoms when a bee flew into my car. It buzzed around before landing on the glass of the passenger window. Carefully, I pressed the button to lower the window so the bee could escape. Instead of thanking me and making a dash for freedom, the startled bee flew to the back of my car and beat its wings against the hot rear glass. If I'd tried to force the bee to follow my directions, it could have turned on me in attack. Instead, I left the windows open and the bee eventually flew to freedom.

Giving advice is like opening a window for someone who is trapped. We can't force her to take the escape routes we point out and it hurts to see her beat her wings against her own wrong choices. Yet we can gently remind her of better options and we can pray for her.

It's like the well-known nursery rhyme, "Humpty Dumpty":

Humpty Dumpty sat on a wall.
Humpty Dumpty had a great fall.
All the king's horses and all the king's men
Couldn't put Humpty together again.

Though the king's men scrambled to help, coax and encourage Humpty, they had to leave Humpty to fry in his own pan. Why couldn't they help? Maybe Humpty was embarrassed to keep trying because he had egg on his face or maybe he just didn't want the help. Whatever the reason, the king's men learned that they couldn't encourage someone who refused to be encouraged. Neither can we.

Letting Go

Sometimes, the best way we can help is to let go. We must realize we don't have the power to change someone's heart, actions or mind.

I learned this lesson when I was in college. I spent the summer of 1976 as the youth director of a small church in Texas. A young woman who was engaged came to see me. "I can't get my boyfriend to get saved!" she said. "I've told him and told him what he needs to do and he won't."

"Perhaps the problem," I reasoned, "is he doesn't want you to make the decision for him. Perhaps you need to tell him you're sorry for trying to force him to follow Christ. Then bow out."

Stella wasn't happy with this advice, but she was desperate enough to give it a try. The results were amazing. Within a matter of hours, Guy reconsidered his decision to receive Christ. Later he said to me, "It was important this be my decision, not one Stella made for me."

Could it be that your rebellious friend or loved one refuses to make a wise choice because she refuses to bow to your will? Perhaps you need to back off and give her permission to make her own choices and even to fail.

Perhaps your loved one needs to struggle. Have you ever watched a baby chick hatch? Although it may be painful to see the chick struggle to break free, you should never try to help by breaking open the shell. If you do, the chick will be too weak to survive. It needs to struggle in order to be strong enough to live. Perhaps we need to allow our sister to struggle so she will be strong enough to fly.

How to Receive Advice

Carolyn Schiedies told me about receiving advice she didn't like. "I was a struggling writer," she said. "I'd sold poems, program material, plays, articles and stories and I was trying to sell a juvenile mystery when my sister-in-law decided I needed to meet her writer-friend neighbor. In the next couple of years, she and I saw each other now and again. One time, we agreed to critique each other's manuscripts. I was careful, afraid to hurt her feelings, afraid to mark up her pristine pages. But she went to work on mine.

"My manuscript came back looking like it had been in a gang war. The poor thing bled from page one. After a large gulp, I sat down and began to read all the corrections, arrows, inserts and comments. A light flashed on. Suddenly, I understood why those rejections kept rolling across my desk.

"She called and rather timidly asked what I thought of her critique. I let her have it—a great big thank-you!

Since then I've had six books published and all because of a friend who cared enough to criticize in love, to tell me the truth about my writing and to actually show me how to do better."

Advice from a friend made a difference to Carolyn because:

- She sought it. This is the important first step, sometimes ignored by those volunteering advice.
- She listened to it. Not everyone who gets good advice is willing to listen. Many would-be authors fail to get through the doors of publishing because they're not willing to learn.
- She evaluated it. Some advice is bad, but a person cannot rely solely on how she feels about it. Just because she doesn't like hearing the advice does not mean it's not good. The listener should think it through with prayer and seek the counsel of God's Word. Unless the advice was meant to hurt, she'll likely find some glimmer of truth if she looks hard enough.
- She followed it. This can be the toughest step to implement. But look at the results Carolyn got by following through. As they use to say in that old Nike ad, "Just do it!"

Eight

Relief for Grief

Carol picked up the ringing telephone. "Hello?"

The voice on the other end was soft. "This is Darla at the nursing home. I'm sorry to tell you, Mrs. Weston, but your mother died in her sleep this morning."

Carol gasped. "Mom's gone?"

Afterward, Carol dialed her best friend, MaryJo, to share the news. But instead of hearing MaryJo's cheery hello, all she heard was a busy signal. Carol's frustration rose as she tried again. Why was it so important she get through? Because Carol was looking for relief and she spelled it M-a-r-y-J-o. But why?

MaryJo couldn't bring Carol's mother back to life, but she could offer a listening ear, wise counsel and perhaps most importantly, she could share Carol's pain.

A half hour later, on the millionth try, MaryJo's phone rang. When Carol heard MaryJo's voice, deep relief swept over her. "Oh, MaryJo, I've been trying to get through to you."

"What's wrong?"

Carol felt the salty sting of tears. Her voice trembled. "The nursing home called. They said Mom slipped away this morning."

"Oh, Carol, I'm so sorry," MaryJo said.

Be There

There is nothing like the shock of the unexpected call that brings bad news. But what do you do when your friend gets such a call? In truth, most people don't know what to do. They feel inadequate to comfort or help. If they were honest, they'd admit bad news makes them feel uncomfortable.

Besides, it hurts to see a friend in grief and to feel her pain. We are a "do it now" society. We want to fix, straighten out and repair broken situations. But when that's not possible, we are left to embrace a friend's heartache and this can make us feel hopeless and helpless.

MaryJo was able to comfort Carol just by being at the other end of the telephone. Let's rewind the scene and watch her respond in slow motion. Do you see her reach for the phone? Do you hear her words? Listen, they're brilliant! She simply says, "I'm so sorry."

Let's listen to what she says next: "Carol, I'll be right over."

Another brilliant remark!

But why would MaryJo want to spend time with Carol? It's obvious she can't fix the situation. Still, MaryJo realizes her presence will give Carol comfort and support. Imagine how Carol would feel if MaryJo decided to keep her distance. What if MaryJo avoided Carol because she didn't feel she had the right words to say? This reaction is what I call the avoidance response.

But when MaryJo arrives at Carol's house, what wise counsel do you think she should offer her friend?

Believe it or not, Carol is not counting on MaryJo's words of wisdom. All Carol really wants is MaryJo's presence, her listening ear and a sympathetic hug or two. Simply being there for a friend is what I call the relief response.

We Need to Be Quiet

What if MaryJo rushed to Carol's side and spent the next hour telling Carol about all the people she's ever known who died in nursing homes? Would this be comforting?

Probably not. Although it might make for interesting conversation a few weeks down the road, but this is not the time to embark on the I-told-you-so, what-did-you-expect? or if-you-think-that-was-bad-let-me-tell-you-this response. After all, Carol is not looking to MaryJo to meet her entertainment needs. Instead, Carol needs time to grieve and time to talk. She does not need stories, guilt or explanations.

Explanations do not make for relief. Sometimes, when we try to explain why a person is in a predicament, we end up hurting the one we are trying to help. Job was a good man who loved God. When his world fell apart, his friends came to sit and grieve with him. This was a great relief response! Unfortunately, they still blew it.

One by one these friends tried to explain to Job why so many calamities had befallen him. I can just picture good-old-Bildad as he slowly stroked his gray beard with one hand and pointed at Job with the other, his brown eyes flashing with judgment, "The reason you have lost your children, flocks and health, Job, is because you are a sinner! You need to repent!"

I don't know about you, but I don't think this is the kind of pep talk Job needed in his time of grief. I'm not the only one who feels this way; this well-meaning explanation did not please the Lord either. After all was said and done, God called Job to pray for his outspoken friends so they could be forgiven. We find this story in Job 42:8-10:

"So now take seven bulls and seven rams and go to my servant Job and sacrifice a burnt offering for yourselves. My servant Job will pray for you, and I will accept his prayer and not deal with you according to your folly. You have not spoken of me what is right, as my servant Job has."

So Eliphaz the Temanite, Bildad the Shuhite and Zophar the Naamathite did what the Lord told them; and the Lord accepted Job's prayer.

After Job had prayed for his friends, the Lord made him prosperous again and gave him twice as much as he had before.

If the response of Job's friends angered God, I guess we'd better watch what we say to those who are hurting! Perhaps we would all be better off if we gave up trying to explain personal tragedies because our explanations often do more harm than good. For example, one pastor I know was told by a disabled man, "The reason you had a Down's syndrome baby is because you weren't sensitive to the handicapped." Another woman was told it was OK her child had died because she had three other children at home.

What kind of comfort is this? Perhaps these people meant well, but their explanations missed the mark. It would have been better if these advisors had kept their mouths closed.

We Need to Share Grief

> "Praise be to the God and Father of our Lord Jesus Christ, the Father of compassion and the God of all comfort, who comforts us in all our troubles, so that we can comfort those in any trouble with the comfort we ourselves have received from God. For just as the sufferings of

> Christ flow over into our lives, so also through Christ our comfort overflows" (2 Corinthians 1:3-5).

According to this Scripture, we are to comfort others. So why do we avoid grieving with friends?

- Their grief makes us feel vulnerable. Some Christians are under the mistaken assumption that bad things don't happen to good people. Ann, a cancer patient, encountered this the moment she told a friend about her illness. "I could see a physical change come over my friend," she said. "Instead of throwing her arms around me, she physically backed away; as if afraid she might somehow become infected with my disease. She was too afraid of her own mortality to face mine."

  Talking to a grieving friend will help you face your fears, Linda Mauer says: "Take time to listen to her describe her pain. This will make it easier for you to continue your relationship. Otherwise, you could shut out a good friend forever."[1]

- Their tragedy revives our unresolved pain. Some of my friends avoided me when my daughter was injured because of unresolved pain in their own lives—grief over a stillborn baby or the death of a parent. Barely coping themselves, exposure to my tragedy dragged them back into unbearable feelings of despair.

  Heidi longed to talk to her mother about her grief after her baby died of sudden infant death syndrome. "But," she said, "every time I brought up Timmy's death, my mother changed the subject. At first, I thought she didn't care. Then I realized she couldn't talk about it. Timmy's death added to the twenty-year grief she'd carried over the death of my brother, Jerry."

Yet talking isn't the only way to communicate grief. Try writing a letter. Explain you feel too close to your own grief to help. Say something like, "I wish I could take away the pain for you, but I can't. Please don't take my silence as rejection but as a friend who is hurting with you."

♥ Their profound struggles shake our faith. When some friends faced our tragedy, they asked, "How could a loving God do this?" Others coped with this same question by not only avoiding us, but by avoiding anyone else who reminded them of what they perceived as God's failure.

After Marcia lost her job, her friend Sharon avoided her. "I knew Marcia was hurting," Sharon said, "but so was I."

After praying for Marcia to be allowed to keep her job, Sharon felt the Lord didn't answer her prayers. "Marcia's pain made me question God and I didn't want to do that."

"Could it be that our heavenly Father permits his children to struggle in order to keep us strong?" James Dobson asks. "I firmly believe this to be true," he says. "That is precisely what James told the Jewish Christians in the first century: 'Consider it pure joy, my brothers, whenever you face trials of many kinds, because you know that the testing of your faith develops perseverance (James 1:2-3)."[2]

Their pain tries our patience. Some people lose patience with a friend caught in the grief process. Tired of seeing the hurt, they want to push past the pain.

Three years after Linda Mauer's eighteen-year-old daughter, Molly, was killed in a train crash in Mexico, friends said they wished Linda and her husband could change back to the way they had been before the accident.

"We can't," Linda says. "Our lives are changed forever. Our friends have to realize that."

In my own ordeal, there were many moments when I wished friends could have plunged in and helped me to shore instead of hanging back, watching me gulp for comfort in pain. How we might have discovered together that churning waters calm when you relax in God. Then we both could have shared the gift of comfort.

We Need to Point Friends to God

Sometimes the best relief or comfort we can provide is to point our friends to God. Karen O'Connor wrote about her friend Dianna: "She had just found out she had breast cancer. I was shocked. Dianna was my dearest friend and had been there for me hundreds of times over the fourteen years we had known one another. Now it was my turn to be there for her during one of her most difficult trials. Yet I felt inadequate.

"'Lord, what can I say that will matter?' I asked. 'Please give me the words.'

"Later that morning, as I was reading my Scripture passage for the day, the heading above 2 Corinthians 1:3-5 caught my attention: 'When troubles come, trust in the God who comforts us.'

"I had my answer. I drew a deep breath and picked up the phone. 'Dianna,' I said with conviction, 'I have some words of encouragement for you, words that matter. God's words.'"

Alene Betts tells another story that shows the impact when we point friends to God. She says, "It was a dreary day for a funeral. Rushing in late, I shook drops off my umbrella and stashed it behind a chair near the door. I was surprised to see the room so full, but it was a fitting tribute. Margaret had lived a full life of ninety-two years.

"Quickly I scanned the room and saw her daughter and son-in-law greeting friends at the foot of the casket. The aroma of flowers and the sound of quiet hymns accompanied soft laughter as guests remembered incidents that knit their lives with the life of a delightful woman. But Anne, Margaret's granddaughter, was nowhere to be found. As she was usually the center of attention, I expected to find her right next to her mom or dad, with her hands turned outward like a kewpie doll.

"Anne was a Down's syndrome young lady who called me her 'spiritual friend.' I found her with her head dropped and lip out. I rushed over and knelt next to her.

"'My grandmother, Margaret; she died,' Anne said.

"'But, Anne, where is she now?' I asked.

"'In that box over there.'

"'Oh, honey, it looks like that, but Anne, your grandmother is with Jesus. It's only her body and clothes that are left behind.'

"Our visit lasted less than five minutes, but Anne's smile was restored. The grief that had poured over her countenance lifted. We walked to the casket and said good-bye.

"Several weeks later an elderly uncle called Anne's mother and said, 'I listened carefully to hear what Alene would tell Anne about the funeral. I was surprised how her words brought Anne from grief to joy.'"

Not only did Alene comfort Anne, her words opened Anne's uncle's eyes. What a beautiful story!

When Relief Made a Difference

It's wonderful to know your encouragement makes a difference. Think how much it means to the one whom you've helped. Kathleen Pace Osborn would agree. She told me, "I was homeward bound on Christmas night in 1996. About a mile from my home, a young woman ran a red light and changed my life forever. In the crash, the seatbelt broke my left collarbone. I was thrown forward with force that broke both bones in my right leg so that they protruded through my skin.

"That crash unleashed, along with seemingly endless difficulties, equally boundless torrents of encouragement. I treasured each morsel. But along with the outpouring of personal touches I received, the encouragement of two strangers, out of nowhere, amazes me most.

"Tessa heard about my situation through my parents' church. She, too, had spent years recovering from extremely serious injuries sustained in an auto accident. Almost as soon as I was released from the hospital, Tessa began to call me. Sometimes it was once a week; often, it was more. She prayed for me. She filled my cup to overflowing with whatever I needed that day, whether it was laughter, shared tears, hope, love or joy. I'm still hurt; she still calls, even though we've never met face to face.

"My other benefactor was George, a man who worked with my best friend, Ilene, in Houston. He took it upon himself to cruise the Internet to find funny poems, jokes and stories to send me. He e-mailed them to Ilene, who then sent them to me. I have stacks of funnies that provide belly laughs rivaling the best medicine. To this day, I've never even spoken to him."

Kathleen is living testimony to what encouragement can do when stirred with time. Isn't it interesting she commends two encouragers whom she's never met? Her story is proof there are things we can do that will help us be there for others, not to take away the pain but to encourage. The following ideas will help you spring into action.

What You Can Do

1. Respect the family's privacy, but be available.

> When making initial contact with a stricken family, be sensitive. Ask if they're ready for guests. If they say no, wait a week or two, then ask again. The first few days of an ordeal are often flooded with well-wishers. Try to maintain contact with the family throughout its struggle. Don't abandon them, even if they say they need a little space from time to time. Keep checking on them and keep inviting them to be with you.

2. If you don't know what to say, say a prayer.

> I found the visitors who meant the most were the ones who told me they prayed for Laura's strength and healing. These prayers washed away my feelings of helplessness and gave me hope to continue my long vigil.

> When Corrine's husband died of a heart attack, a friend told her, "Grief is like surf. It rolls in and out and because of that, I pledge to pray for you every day."

Corrine said some days were so dark she couldn't feel God's presence and wept until she couldn't weep any more. Often she despaired, but then remembered her friend was praying. She later told me, "Knowing prayer was going up for me made all the difference."

3. Be specific in your offer to help.

Many people offered to help after Laura's accident, but I was too grieved to respond. One couple volunteered to have the film from my camera developed. I appreciated this kindness, especially when they returned with beautiful photographs of then eighteen-month-old Laura, taken just prior to the accident.

Mary Sue said, "People helped us in times of illness or crisis with gifts of books, food, time and flowers. Some friends invited us to stay with them after our house fire. We stayed a week, until our realtor gave us her house to live in for six weeks!"

4. Offer to make phone calls or emails, if friends or family need to be notified or updated.

During the weeks following Laura's accident, volunteers kept our friends informed by organizing prayer chains and updating our prayer requests. I appreciated these helpers, as they saved me a lot of time, energy and phone calls. You might make calls to friends of hurting friends to enlist their help. Encourage them to call the family. Ask them to organize meals or make daily grocery trips for milk and bread.

5. Baby-sit and take children on special outings.

   Recently, I saw the sister of a critically ill child at the local mall. It was a joy to watch this girl smile with delight as she rode the merry-go-round. Invite these kids to spend the day, go to the zoo or join your family for pizza. You're apt to brighten the hearts of siblings who are feeling left out or pushed aside.

6. Help with meals.

   Gloria told me, "When a friend was suffering health problems, I invited a mutual friend over to my house to help me cook and freeze meals for her family."

   My mother-in-law brought brown-bag lunches when Laura was in the hospital. Someone sent me a fruit and cheese basket after she was transferred to another hospital. Other friends supplied goodies and home-cooked meals. I encourage this kind of help, but suggest you keep the menu light! I gained ten pounds in the first weeks of Laura's hospital stay.

7. If needed, help raise money.

   Open a bank account and publicize the need. Also, ask if the family needs special equipment that isn't covered by insurance. If so, raise money by hosting a garage sale, a talent show, a church supper or another event. Every little bit helps.

8. Take your friend out for time away.

After spending months in and out of the hospital with a husband in failing health, Kari brought him home and became his primary care provider. She was tired and overwhelmed. A friend called to take her to lunch, arranging for another friend to stay with Kari's husband. Others agreed to watch her husband periodically so Kari could catch up on sleep.

9. Continue concern.

One family told me that although fourteen years have passed since their daughter was released from the hospital, one couple still calls for an update on Sarah's current needs and prayer requests.

10. Send cards of encouragement.

Drop a note to grieving friends from time to time, letting them know you care and that you're praying for them. Don't stop writing, even after the initial crisis is over. Often, in the months that follow a loss, the bereaved need a friend more than ever.

When Sylvia's parents and sister died, she received comforting notes from unexpected people. They comforted with poems, Scripture and personal anecdotes describing a time when they had lost someone close. "It gave me strength," she said.

11. Forgive.

Susan suddenly began to grieve for the baby she'd aborted a decade earlier. In grief, she felt like both a victim and a victimizer. Her friend Jan did not try to argue away Susan's feelings of blame. Instead, she said, "I forgive you and God does too." Because of Jan's words, Susan was finally able to start to forgive herself.

Kate also discovered the power in forgiveness. She lost her sister and four nieces in a Christmas Eve fire. Because of the kinds of questions the firemen asked, Kate concluded that a burning cigarette had triggered the fire. She blamed her brother-in-law, Jake, who often fell asleep while smoking in his easy chair.

Furious, Kate believed Jake had murdered the girls. "Then I realized how much the tragedy had affected him," she said. "In one night, Jake had lost his entire family. I realized it was unfair to let my anger get in the way."

"We have to trust God and let go of our need to strike back," advises Dr. Joe Ehrlich, a Christian psychologist. "Look at Jesus Christ. He was mocked, spit upon, scourged. Yet he yielded his total self to say, 'Father, forgive them' (Lk 23:34). It's not easy, but we need to allow God to use tragic situations to deal with our hearts. This is probably the greatest measurement of how well we are doing in our walk with Christ."[3]

12. Encourage your friend to grieve.

Grief is normal. Expect it. Expect to see it in your bereaved friend for a long time to come. And if you notice your friend is stuffing it inside, suggest she take time to cry. She needs to allow herself time to mourn so she does not become suddenly overwhelmed by emotion. Remember what Jesus said about those who mourn: They shall be comforted (see Mt 5:4). Perhaps he will use us to help perform this task.

When You Need Comfort

Sorrow knocks on everyone's door, sooner or later.

When Sorrow Knocks
By Linda Evans Shepherd

When Sorrow knocked upon my door
I tried to bid her leave.
Instead she sat upon my floor
And there began to weave.
She wove a woe so deep and wide
From streams of anguished tears.
I tried to cast her grief aside;
It tangled in my fears.
Now Sorrow's gone. I'm glad to say
My grief is much relieved.
But, oh, so much I learned the day
That she began to weave.[4]

Sheila told me, "I want to talk to you. I think you may be the only person who understands what I'm going through."

"What's up?" I asked.

Sheila dabbed at her eyes with a tissue. "I have a daughter who is mentally ill," she said. "I've done everything I can to help her, but she's not getting better, she's getting worse. I've prayed and prayed, but my prayers are hitting the ceiling. I still consider myself a Christian, but it seems like God is for everyone else but me."

I said, "I understand how you feel. When Laura was in a coma for a year, I, too, felt cut off from God. But now as I look back over that time period, I can see God's hand was on my life. I was in a season of grief. On the surface, it looked like God was not involved. The sod seemed frozen, but it was in the warm depths that God was working—where I could not see."

Our lives are made of changing seasons. But seasons of grief and suffering often seem overwhelming. With no hope for relief, the waiting can seem to last forever.

When my dad was a boy, he planted a peanut patch. On the surface, it looked like nothing was happening, so he dug up his crop. Of course, the peanuts, which had been developing all along, stopped developing after that. But Dad learned that growth and change are taking place even when we cannot see them.

My friend with the mentally ill daughter is in a season of waiting. Though she prays, hopes and suffers, she cannot see the results—because they are happening beneath the surface. Her inability to see, however, does not mean God is not working. When we are having problems coping with suffering, we need to practice the GRIEF Relief Principle:

Grief:

G	Give it to God.
R	Remember, this isn't heaven yet.
I	Improve time with God.
E	Expect trauma to take time to heal.
F	Forgive yourself, others and God.

Relief:
Remember, God cares and shares your pain.

G: Give it to God.

Remember, God is the giver of all good gifts. He can use our tragedies for good. He says all things work together for the good of those that love the Lord and are called according to his purpose (see Rom 8:28). But God does not do bad things to us so he can use them for his glory. He does not step on us or mangle us beneath the wheels of tragedy.

Jesus used the sad circumstance of a man born blind to open the eyes of other people. He didn't gouge the man's eyes out and say, "Great, now I can heal you!" Instead, he healed eyes that had been blind from birth. He opened the spiritual eyes of others by opening the eyes of a man born blind (see Jn 9:1-41).

Before God can turn suffering into something good, we have to give the situation to him. The blind man submitted to Christ's authority. We need to do the same thing by repeatedly praying, "I give my situation to you, God. Please take it from my shoulders and carry it for me."

R: Remember, this isn't heaven yet.

The characters on TV sitcoms are always able to resolve their problems within thirty minutes. If the star of your favorite show dies, that's OK—it was only a dream sequence anyway. Even characters who are riddled with bullets are always sufficiently recovered to star in the next episode.

It's too bad real life isn't like that. Not only is this life not a TV sitcom, it is also not yet heaven! As long as we are still on this earth, we have to contend with sorrow, injustice and loss. This means we will, at some time or another, be called upon to struggle. Unfortunately, we may never see a purpose to our suffering and perhaps that's the point.

Maybe we should take our lessons from Job. Do you realize God never told Job why he suffered? God wanted Job to trust him in spite of and through his circumstances. Otherwise, Job might have loved God only for what he could get.

And how did Job finally respond to God's silence? I think his response is one of the most beautiful Scriptures in the Bible: "Though he slay me, yet will I hope in him" (Jb 13:15).

What was the result of such faith, patience and devotion? At the end of the story, Job was a richer man, both spiritually and materially. He had talked with God face to face. Wow! Although God never answered his demand to know why, Job felt closer to his maker.

After all, Proverbs 3:5 says: "Lean not on your own understanding."

That's good advice! We can hope in God in the midst of pain.

I: Improve time with God.

Seeking God is eventually what brought me relief in the midst of my pain. It was in my quest that I learned to pray and spend time in the Word. My growing relationship with God brought me comfort despite my circumstances.

E: Expect trauma to take time to heal.

The grief cycle can take years. We need to manage our pain in small bites so that we are not choked by emotion. We can't expect too much too soon. We need to be patient and learn it's OK to grieve. It is not OK to stifle grief. This could result in damage to our health. Instead of holding back, we need to work through our tears, anger, sorrow and all the other crazy feelings that may surface. We will get through it if we take one day at a time.

F: Forgive yourself, others and God.

Since it may take years to get over a major loss, we may switch from grief to anger to blame. Some of our anger may even be directed at God. We need to be patient with ourselves and continually seek to break through the anger and forgive!

Forgive Who?

Yourself—If you're placing blame, real or imagined, for your loss on yourself, you may not be able to argue the blame away. Ask God to give you the power to forgive yourself and ask him to help others to forgive you as well.

Others—This can be tough, but it can be accomplished. The way I get through deep bitterness toward others is to pray, "Lord, I'm willing to forgive, but I'm not strong enough. Even so, I give you permission to forgive this person through me." Afterward, I may not feel warm and fuzzy toward the person with whom I'm angry, but that's OK. I find the feelings will eventually follow—someday.

Pray this prayer as often as you need to, even every ten minutes. When you do, you will find God is able, moment by moment, to give you strength to accomplish even the impossible. If you're not yet ready to pray in this way, pray God will bring you to the point where you can. He will, in his own time.

God—He may not have authored your suffering, but you may still be angry with him for allowing it. That's OK. He's big enough to take it. But you don't want to let your anger break off communication with him. Tell him how you feel. He knows anyway. Then say something like, "God, I want to forgive you. Help me to forgive."

When you're able to let go of your anger at God, you will find God is able and willing to help you work through your grief.

Relief: Jesus' Response to Tragedy

Remember the story of Lazarus? While Jesus was away from Jerusalem, Lazarus' sisters sent word their brother was at the point of death. The sisters knew if Jesus returned to town in time, he would heal their brother with a miraculous touch. Can you imagine how they must have felt when Jesus delayed? As their brother died in their arms, they must have cried out, "Jesus, where are you?"

Four days after they laid Lazarus in his tomb, Jesus showed up. Martha saw him coming and ran to him, falling at his feet. "Lord," she cried, "if you had been here, my brother would not have died." (Jn 11:32).

What was Jesus' reaction? He knew he was about to call Lazarus forth from the grave, from death into life. Yet he did a curious thing. He wept. Can you imagine that? As Martha lay sobbing at his feet, tears ran down Jesus' cheeks. Why? He wept because it hurt to see Mary and Martha in such emotional pain.

I believe it still hurts him to see us grieve for the loss of one we love. I believe he weeps with us and longs to help carry our pain. This is relief, because no matter what our circumstances are, he cares and is with us. We are never alone.

The Benefits of Suffering

What did Job gain from his tragedy? Pain, heartache and loss. But he also grew to know God better, appreciated life more, and was thankful for his new family and the wealth God restored to him. He survived his time of struggling and was stronger spiritually and learned to trust God, despite his circumstances.

What does God give us when we suffer?

- ♥ Comfort
- ♥ Wisdom
- ♥ Faith
- ♥ Patience
- ♥ Trust
- ♥ Love
- ♥ Hope

Remember, whenever God allows us to be burdened with grief, he will put his arms underneath, to help us carry the load.

Nine

Turn for Good

"Do unto others as you would have them do unto you."

Most of us can quote the Golden Rule. But what does it mean? Does it mean we should do to get? Does it mean I should do something kind to get a like response? I don't think so. Simply put, it means we should be kind.

How do we do that? How do we practice, as the bumper stickers and popular books advise us, "random acts of kindness"? Perhaps we need to look for opportunities to serve. This is exactly what Ruth Smeltzer meant when she said, "You have not lived a perfect day, even though you have earned your money, unless you have done something for someone who will never be able to repay you."[1]

When Kindness Helps

Does kindness make a difference in the lives of others? Absolutely. I'm always touched, grateful and humbled when someone goes out of his or her way to do me a good turn. In our fast-paced society, it takes time and planning to perform a conscientious act for a friend or a stranger. That's why, when I receive a good deed, I stand up and take notice.

One day, I had the pleasure of receiving a good deed with my Big Mac and fries. It was dark when I pulled my blue Taurus up to a drive-thru window at a McDonald's in Boulder, Colorado. My then nine-year-old son and I were weary and hungry after spending two hours driving through winding mountain roads. I handed the cashier my twenty-dollar bill so when he handed back my steaming food, I pulled forward to allow the next car in line access to the window while I fumbled with the straws. Suddenly, I was aware of a person hovering over my still-open window. I looked up to see the eyes of the friendly cashier. He breathlessly gushed, "You forgot your change."

I broke into a wide grin. "Oh! Thanks so much!"

The young man had gone out of his way to bring a forgetful lady her change. Why was I so impressed? Because his action expressed honesty and caring. Not only did he care about doing a good job, he cared about his customer. That made me feel proud and grateful for him. This may be no big thing, but it shows the impact a simple act of kindness can make. It tells me a good turn is worth the trouble and the potential embarrassment.

One afternoon, I was sitting at the kitchen table in a home in the mountain town of Frisco, Colorado. Gray clouds hung over rocky, tree-swept slopes. I listened to the wind as it blew flurries of sparkling snow off the white drifts left from previous storms. As I stared at the gray sky, I saw a strange sight. A black, shrouded figure appeared about a hundred feet above the ground. It circled above a neighboring home, flapping its cape. I laughed out loud and pointed it out to my son. "What is that?" I asked.

His eyes grew big. "It looks like a witch flying on her broom."

"I think the wind picked some object off the ground and is slinging it through the sky." We both laughed as we watched the flapping silhouette disappear in the direction of the park. "Let's see if we can find it," I suggested.

Snuggled into our down coats and winter boots, we stomped the two blocks through crusty snow to the park. On the baseball diamond we found our "witch." It turned out to be a state-of-the-art tent, wadded in a heap of poles and blue and green nylon.

"I bet someone is going to miss this," I said.

Young Jimmy nodded. "Do you think we could find its owner?"

"We could try. It had to have come from someplace near here."

As we walked down the street, dragging the tent, I saw a man working on his car. "Does this tent belong to you?" I inquired.

The man looked at me, dumbfounded. "Nope. Where'd you get it?"

"It blew into the park," I explained.

"Hey, don't try to find the owner," he reasoned. "Consider it a gift of luck. That's a nice tent."

After conferring with Jimmy, we decided to press on. The man must have thought we had stepped out of Oz as we rang the door of the next house. A young woman answered, her small boys peeking out from behind her. I blurted, "Does this tent belong to you? We saw it sailing around the neighborhood and found it over in the park."

Her eyes widened. "That's my husband's tent! We had it set up in the backyard to air it out."

"It's been on quite an adventure," I told her.

"If only you knew," she said. "This tent has even been to Nepal and back. It's like a member of our family. My husband would have been devastated if we had lost it."

The man across the street shook his head as he saw us give the woman the tent. Too bad I couldn't explain how exciting it was to have done this good turn or the warmth we felt, watching her children jump with glee as they dragged the tent into their garage. As we trudged home, we giggled at the excitement we had witnessed. Perhaps we had given this family the gift of a returned tent. But they had given us something, too—satisfaction and a glow from the inside out.

When to Be Kind

There are opportunities all around us to do good deeds. Sometimes we recognize them and sometimes we don't. All too often, we let them pass by because we're afraid to get involved. When Laura was eight years old, she spent a week at Children's Hospital recovering from a bladder infection which had infected her bloodstream. How relieved we were when her condition was downgraded from critical and she was able to leave the ICU for a regular room.

During the crisis, I spent every waking moment at the hospital or in a nearby hotel room. My husband had been relegated to caring for six-year-old Jimmy. The day before Easter, he brought Jimmy to see his sister. I couldn't help but smile as I watched my little boy proudly carry a basket of colorful eggs that he and his daddy had decorated. As he passed children wheeling themselves down the hall in their wheelchairs, he would reach down to take a single egg. "Would you like an Easter egg?" he asked each child. I beamed, misty-eyed. I couldn't believe my son was giving away his own Easter eggs.

Later, as we got onto the elevator to go to the snack room, I panicked. A sad young woman stood next to us. I could tell she was in deep pain, probably grieving over a seriously ill child. I looked down at my son and fear gripped my heart. I could tell he was going to offer one of his eggs to this sad mother. I wanted to whisper, "Jimmy, please leave this lady alone." But the words froze in my throat as I watched him carefully lift an egg from his basket. "Would you like an Easter egg?" he asked, blue eyes shining.

The sad young woman looked down at him. Her eyes filled with tears as she gasped, "Thank you. This will be the only Easter egg my son will get this year." My eyes misted too, as pride replaced my panic. My small son's act of kindness had warmed a heart.

I began to realize that I, too, needed to be more open to reaching out to others. The results would be worth any personal embarrassment I might temporarily feel. This experience my son and I shared reminds me of a poem I penned:

Day's End

Because I'll not repeat this day,
I'll leave good deeds along my way.
If I may give a word that's kind,
No sad regrets I'll leave behind.
If I may calm a baby's cry,
If I may stop to dry an eye,
If I may pause to show I care,
I'll know I made a difference there.
And when the day is at its end,
I'll know I spent it well, my friend.

This poem is a great reminder that today is the day to show a kindness, for tomorrow may be too late.

How to Be Kind

Recently a quote that came in over the Internet made me laugh. It seems eight-year-old Carolyn explained marriage this way: “My mother says to look for a man who is kind... That’s what I’ll do....I’ll find somebody who’s kinda tall and handsome.”

Well, I’m not certain Carolyn has a good grip on what kindness really is. The New Expanded Webster’s Dictionary defines kindness as, “Quality or state of being kind; benevolence, a kind act.”

The apostle John gives an even better definition of kindness: “Dear children, let us not love with words or tongue but with actions and in truth” (1 Jn 3:18).

This means we need to put action to our love. Here are some suggestions for kind things we can do for others. Remember, the best acts are the ones done in love.

Pitch in to help.
Supply a need.
Give an unexpected surprise.
Spend time listening or counseling.

What to Expect

As we discussed, we don’t do to get. If our motive for a kindness is some sort of payback, we are operating from the wrong spirit. This kind of motivation reminds me of Zelda who grew up in a small town fifty years ago. She married a farmer and her days were spent chasing her small daughter and cooking meals in the kitchen of their farmhouse. The only excitement Zelda found was dreaming about winning the contests she often entered. Her husband was a good man, but the years were kind neither to his hair nor to his waistline. One day, Zelda got a call. She’d won a trip for her entire family to New York City!

When the family arrived in New York, they walked into the lobby of a fine hotel. While her husband was checking in at the front desk, Zelda and her daughter took a look around. What Zelda saw next nearly knocked her socks off. An old, decrepit man in a wheelchair rolled himself to a shiny wall and pressed a button.

"What's that?" her daughter asked.

"I don't know," Zelda admitted. "Let's watch and see what happens."

She stared in amazement as the wall slid open and the old man wheeled himself inside. The wall slid shut and circular lights blinked one direction, then the other. As they stared, the wall slid open. Out strolled a distinguished and handsome man. Zelda turned to her daughter. "What a wonderful contraption! Let's get your pa to try it."

Zelda was disappointed. The results she'd hoped for were not to be. She expected her husband to be made dramatically more handsome by the act of entering an elevator.

Perhaps you're hoping your acts of kindness will dramatically change your loved ones. You may be hoping they will have a better attitude or see you in a better light. Maybe they will, but you could be disappointed too. That's why love should always be your motivation, no strings attached. Then, regardless of the reaction your deed may provoke, you will find satisfaction can't be taken away from you.

Squelch the Impulse to Be Unkind

Despite the best intentions, there are times when we may not feel like being kind: when your boss loses his or her temper, your children break grandmother's antique vase or someone steals your parking space. Let's face it, sometimes we feel like being rude! But we need to recall the words of

Paul:

> "Make sure that nobody pays back wrong for wrong, but always try to be kind to each other and to everyone else" (1 Thessalonians 5:15).
>
> I guess Paul was able to pen this because he was self-employed, had no children and didn't drive a car! Even so, we need to fight the urge for revenge. Don't tempt regrets—be nice when others aren't. Otherwise, you may find yourself as embarrassed as Sally Ann, who was running late for an important business meeting. Not only did she burn her toast, but her husband decided that morning would be a good day to lecture her about her toothpaste habits. The two got into a terrific argument. Later, when Sally Ann asked Jeff to zip up her red power dress, he said, "I'll show you zipping!" and whipped the zipper up and down until it was hopelessly jammed.

After cutting herself out of her most expensive dress, Sally Ann quickly changed into her gray suit, buttoned up the front and hurried out the door.

That evening, arriving home from work, she walked through the garage and found her husband under the car with his legs sticking out. Frazzled and still angry at him, she said, "I'll show you zipping!" She reached down and gave his zipper a few good yanks.

Once in the kitchen, she was shocked to see her husband preparing a large salad. She gasped, "Jeff, who's in the garage?"

"Our neighbor, Carl. He's taking a look at my brakes."

"Oh no!" Sally Ann shrieked. She told Jeff what she'd done and he went with her to the garage to help her apologize.

When they called Carl's name, he didn't respond. When they finally dragged him out from under the car, he was unconscious and bleeding from slamming his head each time he got zipped.

Remember: Temper, temper; zip it before it flies!

So, in other words, keep a soft answer ready when someone yells at you. Hug the child who breaks your favorite vase. Wave (in a friendly manner) at the person who steals your parking place. "A gentle answer turns away wrath" (Proverbs 15:1).

How to Accept Kindness

It's not always easy to accept a kindness. In fact, there are times when accepting a kindness means you need to humble yourself. What is the best way to accept a kindness? Graciously. A simple "thank you," a note or a kindness in return are appropriate expressions.

I remember a time when I did not want to accept a kindness. My husband and I had flown to the tiny Caribbean island of Dominica for a short vacation. In the mornings, we dove offshore amidst the beautiful tropical fish while the afternoons were reserved for exploring the island. One afternoon, Paul and I decided to hike to a waterfall fed by hot springs. When we got to the trail, we found it really wasn't a hike but more like a wild rock scramble. The going was difficult at times because the terrain was wet and some of the rocks were slick with moss.

A young man joined Paul and me and, despite our protests, insisted he guide us up the falls. Paul and I wanted to be self-sufficient; after all, we were graduates of the Colorado Mountain School and we knew how to hike up a trail and scramble over rocks. I soon began to realize how valuable the guide's assistance was, however, as he helped me cross a small river. My leg muscles were still shaky after my attempt to hike ten miles the day before and they didn't always respond the way I wanted.

The falls were beautiful. As we sat beneath the gushing spout, the hot water and rocks felt good to my sore muscles. On the way down, the guide showed me the safest places to put my feet. Suddenly a rock caught the edge of my hiking boot as I stepped onto a cliff and I began to fall backward. The guide turned and grabbed my hand, keeping me from plummeting headfirst to the jagged rocks below.

How grateful I was. Of course, the guide's motivation was to earn a nice tip, but he provided a wonderful service. He saved my life. So be careful before you shoo away someone's kindness. God may have put that person in your life for a reason. Accept it with grace and when you get a chance, return the favor to someone else.

TEN

Earnest Prayer Warms the Heart

Recently, after I spoke at a Mothers of Preschoolers (MOPS) meeting, I joined a discussion group. Betty Jean lamented, “When I was working, I used to be envious of stay-at-home mothers. That must be the life, I thought as I compared my hectic workday with what I thought their days were like.

“I couldn’t wait until my first baby arrived, believing our days would be filled with warm and tender moments. I would finally get my house organized and have time for occasional napping. Nobody told me what motherhood was really like. I’m isolated with a fussy baby and piles of laundry, I’m miserable.”

Ruthie agreed, “I feel the same way. I thank God for my healthy baby. But motherhood has been a transition. Besides, we’ve recently moved here from out of state. I feel so alone.”

“I feel alone, too,” Melissa added. “My husband and I are only here for a few more weeks. I miss my friends in California. I’ve written volumes of letters, but no one has replied. When I call, they say, ‘I got you a birthday card, but I haven’t sent it yet.’” Her eyes brimmed with tears. “My birthday was two months ago.” She looked down at her hands as her voice dropped. “Not only that, but motherhood hasn’t been what I had thought it would be.”

“It will get easier,” Ruthie said.

Melissa looked up. “My baby is so fussy. I can’t go back to sleep when she wakes me up at night and my mother-in-law is visiting. She thinks the baby’s adorable, but she will hardly speak to me. I feel so alone.”

Connie, the discussion leader, said, “Call and remind us to pray for you.”

“Why wait?” I challenged. “Let’s pray for Melissa now. Is there anyone else here who needs encouragement through prayer?”

One by one the hands went up and soon our circle of young mothers bowed their heads. As we prayed, I could hear soft sniffles. Afterward, tissues came out to wipe mascara-stained cheeks.

“I feel so encouraged,” Melissa said, with a soft smile.

Other women nodded their heads. “We should pray for one another more often,” Betty Jean said.

“And exchange phone numbers since we’re all going through the same things!” Connie added.

Like Connie, we tend to put off prayer, sometimes indefinitely. Yet there is no more powerful form of encouragement. I found this to be true when I hosted an online chat for teenagers desperate to discuss their problems.

"My dad came home drunk again," one wrote.

"I'm thirteen and sleeping with my boyfriend," typed another.

"I think I'm addicted to drugs," responded a third.

What I discovered was even if I could give these teens the best advice in the world, I could not touch their hearts until I prayed for them then and there.

Prayer Can Reach People

Can prayer open doors, introducing friends and family to a loving God? Absolutely! At one retreat where I spoke, Janie shared the following story.

"One day I was walking by my boss's office and I saw him reach for his receiver to take a phone call. As I was walking away, he began to yell and scream.

"I ran back to Jack's office and found him on the floor, quaking in convulsions. I picked up the fallen receiver to discover the caller had just informed Jack his wife had been killed in a head-on collision.

"Other coworkers gathered around our stricken boss, but no one knew what to do. I knew he didn't believe in God, yet I knelt down and said, 'I think we need to pray.'

"I placed my hand on Jack's shoulder and asked for God's peace and comfort."

Janie said later her coworkers told her how much they admired her for what she did. Even Jack, when he recovered, thanked Janie for the prayer that day.

Prayer is always appropriate in times of crisis. Your prayers for friends and family not only touch God but may be the thing needed to point those for whom you pray to his forgiveness and love.

The Difference Prayer Can Make

If you have been on the receiving end of prayer, you know what a difference it can make. Speaker Pam Bianco says, "During a time of major crises in my life and ministry, I needed help—not the everyday kind, but the prayer-warrior, stretcher-bearer kind. God sent three women to pray for me. With their separate but interwoven encouragement, I have retained a biblical perspective that diminished the effects of hurt and bitterness in my life. By bearing my stretcher through prayer, they brought me to the one who healed my hurt. Because of their love, these three friends will always remain special to me."

I have witnessed prayer's power, not only when others have prayed for me but also when I have prayed for others. I shared with you about my daughter's hospitalization as she recovered from a critical bladder infection. The Lord used our time at the hospital to enable me to give back some of the prayer encouragement I had received previously.

One day, as I stood by Laura's bed talking to the charge nurse, the unit secretary interrupted. "There's a mom in the hallway crying hysterically," she said. "Is there anything we can do?"

The nurse shook her head sadly. I realized her time was dedicated to the needs of her small patients. She did not have time to comfort their parents.

This news piqued my interest, however. A mom crying in the hallway?! I have to investigate, I decided, watching the secretary walk back to her office.

I slipped out of the unit and there in the hall, I found a young Chinese mother on her knees, weeping. I had seen her earlier in the ICU, hovering over the limp body of her tiny daughter, who was hooked to tubes and beeping monitors.

I knelt beside Annie. "May I pray for you?" I asked.

She looked up at me with teary eyes. "Would you?"

I could feel her body tremble with sobs as I put my arm around her shoulders.

Squeezing my eyes closed, I prayed, "Lord, Annie's journey is so hard, yet I know you're with her. I thank you she's not alone. Let Annie feel your presence. Put your arms around her and let her know you care. Be with her daughter and help her to recover."

I could feel Annie's sobs subside. I opened my eyes and gently asked, "Annie, what's wrong with your little girl?"

Tears of pain gathered in the corners of Annie's eyes. "She's profoundly handicapped," was all she managed to whisper.

I nodded in understanding and patted her shoulder. I bowed my head again. "God, Annie's daughter is a special gift. Thank you that this little one's life will bring joy and blessings, just as my daughter's life has brought me joy and blessings. Be with this mother and this child and teach them how to find you in every situation. In Jesus' name, Amen."

Annie looked up and smiled through tears. "Thank you so much for praying," she said. "I feel peace now."

I was delighted Annie felt at peace, but the funny thing was, I felt at peace too. I had just been in God's presence and felt his comfort flow through me to Annie. I could only marvel at his faithfulness.

When to Pray

When should we pray? The apostle Paul says it this way:

> "Pray continually" (1 Thes 5:17).

I think this verse means we should be in constant dialogue with God, commenting on the events around us and asking for strength, intervention and wisdom. This doesn't mean we should go through life praying with our eyes closed. Instead, we should go through life praying with our eyes open, praying about what we see around us.

Do you remember the last time you were in the grocery store and saw a tired woman juggling a basket of groceries while trying to calm a screaming child? Even if you merely saw your own reflection, your response should be the same. You should pray! Say something like, "Lord, I know you see that woman over there. Would you give her strength to help her make it through the day? Would you let her know you love her?"

Perhaps your nine-year-old son shows up with a bad grade on his spelling test. You could pray, "Lord, give me wisdom to help my son and not lose my temper."

Let's say your best friend calls to tell you her husband has lost his job. This time, instead of praying silently, pray out loud. "Lord, be with Lisa and George. Help them during this time. Comfort Lisa, strengthen George and meet their daily needs. Help George to find work soon."

Now that's what I call praying continually!

We should also pray as God leads. Have you ever been worried about a friend? Perhaps that's God's way of prompting you to pray for her! It is important to recognize and not neglect these promptings.

One woman told me about being overwhelmed with feelings of suicide late one night. Although she decided to swallow a bottle of pills, she changed her mind. She was surprised to get a phone call from a friend the next morning. "Priscilla, what was going on with you last night?" Peg exclaimed. "God woke me up and wouldn't let me go back to sleep until I prayed for you. Is everything OK?"

Priscilla was stunned. God did care! He had intervened. He had called Peg to prayer on her behalf! This goes to show how important it is to pray when we feel his gentle nudge.

One November day, my family and I were flying our small plane when we had airplane trouble. Acidic smoke filled the cockpit. We worried about fire and looked for a clearing in the thick Louisiana pine forest to make an emergency landing. I silently cried out, “Lord, don’t you have anyone praying for us?”

Immediately, I pictured my friend Linda Deeming, her head bowed in prayer. “Is Linda praying for us, Lord?” I asked in wonder.

Fortunately, the smoke cleared and our terrifying plane ride had a happy landing. And several days after our gentle glide down the runway, I e-mailed Linda, asking, “Did you happen to pray for me last Friday?”

Linda sent back the message: “Funny you should ask. The Lord woke me up at eleven o’clock Thursday night and called me to prayer. I sat up in bed and prayed until five in the morning. Finally I felt a peace and was able to go back to sleep. I didn’t know whom I was praying for; all I knew was somebody was in danger. What happened?”

Wow! To think God would prompt someone to pray for me and my family for six hours, even before we faced the crisis in the cockpit. How grateful I am to God for helping us land safely. I’m also grateful he called Linda to pray and that she obediently answered his call.

Besides spontaneous prayer and following God’s nudging to pray, we can pencil in a regular prayer time on our calendars. Many people like to rise early, use a coffee break or wait until a quiet moment to spend time with God in prayer, devotional study and Bible reading. A pad and pencil will help you list people for whom you’re praying. When your prayers are answered, it’s exciting to note your praise as a reminder of how good God is.

How to Pray

Prayer is actual conversation with a God who cares. Yet, I think we sometimes forget to whom we are talking. We are like the group of farmers who met in the local church to pray for rain. As they prayed, a small boy tugged at his dad's sleeve.

"Yes?" the farmer asked, looking down at the lad.

"Dad, if we are praying for rain, why didn't we bring an umbrella?"

That's a good question. We need to expect God to answer our prayers. After all, he's listening.

The rules of prayer are simple. To pray, we simply talk to God, just as we would talk to a friend. We can tell him about our day, request petitions or even complain! Complaining is OK because God wants us to take our burdens and leave them with him so as to lighten our load.

I think the biggest obstacle to prayer is that we forget. We need reminders like a daily prayer time penciled on a calendar, a to-do list, sticky notes or whatever it takes. One woman told me that when she prays for someone, she writes the name down on the palm of her hand as a constant reminder. She says that's how God thinks of us. The prophet Isaiah wrote:

"See, I have engraved you on the palms of my hands; your walls are ever before me."

Isaiah 49:16

When it comes to encouraging others, the most important thing we can do is offer our requests to God on their behalf. Praying for friends reminds me of this poem.

I Said a Prayer for You Today
Author Unknown

I said a prayer for you today—
And know God must have heard.
I felt the answer in my heart—
Although he spoke no word.
I didn't ask for wealth or fame—
I knew you wouldn't mind.
I asked him to send treasures
Of a far more different kind.
I asked that he'd be near you
At the start of each new day
To grant you health and blessings
And friends to share your way.
I asked for happiness for you
In all things great and small.
But it was for his loving care
I prayed the most of all.

Wouldn't it be nice if someone prayed like that for you today? And wouldn't it be a gift if you prayed like that for someone else?

Give It to God

When we are worried about a loved one, the best thing we can do is to give him or her to God through prayer. Karen O'Connor shared this wonderful story: "Some years back, I was frantic with worry over my then twenty-year-old son. His father and I had been recently divorced and he was upset, feeling displaced and terribly hurt. Stuck in turmoil, he smoked pot, lived out of his car for a time, hung out with other irresponsible young people and generally sank deeper and deeper into his pain. He had been living with his dad at the time and things were not going well between them.

"One morning, at a women's prayer group, I couldn't contain my tears or my fears, any longer. I broke down in front of the entire room, sobbing with frustration, anger, guilt, regret and remorse. I wanted to do something for my hurting son, but I didn't know what.

"Within seconds of my speaking, an older women walked across the room, sat beside me and put her arm around me. 'Hush,' she said sweetly, stroking my hair as she would a child's. 'Your parenting in the flesh is over. This is between your son and his father. Stand back. Let them work it out. Your parenting now must be in the spirit. Pray,' she said. 'Never stop praying for your son. And leave the results to the Lord.' An unexpected peace came over me in that moment. I knew she was right. I knew what I had to do and I began doing it—every day.

"My life turned around that day and in the years since, so has my son's—all because of one woman's encouraging words."

What a testimony to the power of prayer. Yet, interceding for another is no easy task. Sometimes when we are interceding, we hold on to our burden too tightly. We have to learn how to seek God, then lay our burdens at his feet. There is only one way to do that and that's to ask God to help us let go. This does not mean we stop praying; it means we learn to trust God with the results, regardless of whether things go the way we want them to go.

Sometimes, when I'm wrestling with a burden, I will lay it down at God's feet, then pick it up again. At other times I find I have to relinquish a burden several times a day but that's OK. This only means God is at work, gently coaxing me to let go. Whether or not I get the outcome I desire, God will use the situation for his good purpose.

Sometimes God surprises me. The thing I'm fighting so hard to convince God to change is often the very thing God uses to accomplish the prayer of my heart. Isn't that just like him? We have to remember that in the end, God's way is always the best way. That's where we find joy, relief and release.

How to Pray for Yourself

When I speak publicly, I like to make my audiences laugh by telling them my favorite prayer is, "Help!" The only thing is I'm not joking. I rely on God's help to get me through each day. If you were to come into my home, you would find me juggling too many batons in the air despite the fact I can't juggle! I have to rely on the Lord to not only keep me balanced, but to keep from stumbling.

Perhaps you're like me. You have many responsibilities: spouse, children, home, job. Face it, we women are all jugglers and the "Help!" prayer is a good one for each and every one of us. But we need to move beyond this cry and seek God as our Savior, Lord, friend and counselor. He's all of this and more.

The best way to approach God is with hands full. If you have avoided him because you did not want him to see you were carrying around bitterness, anger, jealousy or impure thoughts, I have good news for you. He already knows you're carrying those things and loves you anyway. He wants you to come to him just as you are, even if your hands are filled with the slime of sin. But you need to lay your sin down, right at his feet and he will restore your soul.

Let's say you're struggling with unforgiveness. Tell him, "Lord, I'm mad at my husband, again. I'm fed up with __________ (fill in the blank) and I wish I could make him pay for what he did. Lord, please forgive me. Help me to let go of my bitterness. I lay it at your feet. In your Son's precious name."

The reason you want to pray something like this is because God is a holy God. Although he accepts you just as you are, you will have a hard time growing deeper in relationship with him if you refuse to come clean. Ask him to reveal any dirt you may have overlooked. When he reveals it, you need to confess it to clean up your act.

God enjoys a child with a pure heart. If you've ever pulled a sweet-smelling baby out of a tub of soapy water, you will know what I'm talking about. When we come clean before God, we can have that special time of sweet fellowship. Before you close your prayer, don't forget to thank him for all he has done for you.

Now that you have approached him, clean from your spiritual bath, make your requests known to him. Cry out about your concerns. Tell him about your problems and implore him for his help and strength. When you close your prayer, leave your burden with him.

I like to pray something like this:

> "Lord, I give you my burden of __________. I lay it at your feet. Give me the power to trust you with this situation. In Jesus' name, Amen."

Whenever you pray in this manner, you will find your burdens lighter and your way brighter. After all, you have sought the encouragement of the God of the universe, the God who loves you.

Eleven

Nice Words

I love a story Florence Littauer shares. One Sunday morning, speaking to a church she called the children forward and had them sit around her. “This morning I’m going to teach you one verse that I taught my children,” she said. “It is Ephesians 4:29: ‘Let no corrupt communication proceed out of your mouth, but that which is good to the use of edifying, that it may minister grace unto the hearers.’”

The children were baffled by some of the big words and Florence took time to explain: “When words come out of our mouths,” she said, “they should be like little presents all wrapped up to be given away.”

Florence tells what happened next: “One precious little girl stood up, stepped into the aisle and said loudly to the whole congregation, as if serving as my interpreter,

'What she means is that our words should be like little silver boxes with bows on top."[1]

I love the way Florence and her young interpreter expressed this idea. Our words of encouragement are meant to be gifts of love, packaged attractively.

Wrong Words

Our words can be gifts of love or they can be fiery darts of hate. We should be careful before carelessly tossing acid words at others. Proverbs 4:24 states plainly: "Put away perversity from your mouth; keep corrupt talk far from your lips." If you follow this Scripture, you will more than likely stay out of trouble.

This reminds me of a story I once heard about a parrot who had a problem with perverse talk. It seems a quiet Christian woman bought this beautiful macaw at her local pet store. The shop's owner assured her, "Pierre will be the perfect companion for you and he has an incredible vocabulary."

When Velma brought Pierre home, she discovered to her horror that her pet swore like a sailor. Velma was a patient woman and hoped she could teach the bird right from wrong, but the more she tried to convince Pierre to clean up his talk, the more he swore. After many sleepless nights, poor Velma had heard enough. Early one morning, when the bird began his angry tirade, peppering the house with foul words, Velma stumbled out of bed, bleary-eyed and angry. She grabbed the parrot and shut him in the kitchen cabinet.

The bird kicked and clawed, swearing louder than ever.

In desperation, Velma opened the door, pulled the bird out, then shoved him into the freezer. For the first few seconds, there was a terrible hullabaloo. The bird shrieked, kicked and clawed. Suddenly, all was quiet.

Velma stared at the freezer, then realized her bird might be hurt. Panicked, she threw open the door. Pierre calmly climbed onto Velma's outstretched arm and said, "Awfully sorry about the trouble I gave you, Madam. I'll do my best to improve my vocabulary from now on."

Velma was astounded at the transformation that had come over her parrot—that is, until he asked, "By the way, what did the chicken do?"

The ill-tempered parrot cleaned up his beak-speak. He was learning the wisdom of Proverbs 10:19: "When words are many, sin is not absent, but he who holds his tongue is wise."

We might all take a lesson from Pierre. There are times when we should hold our tongues and refrain from saying words we will later regret. There are also times to loosen the tongue and say words of hope, encouragement, cheer and comfort. "Pleasant words are a honeycomb, sweet to the soul and healing to the bones," says Proverbs 16:24.

The Difference Our Words Can Make

One kind word goes a long way in encouraging others. It can make a difference in ways we can't imagine. Writing coach and editor Susan Titus Osborn found this to be true at a surprise reunion. She told me, "Exhausted from a busy morning, I walked into the luncheon at a large convention and scanned the room for an empty seat. Suddenly a woman hurried to me, clasped my hand, smiled and said, 'Susan, how wonderful to see you!'

"I smiled back and quickly glanced at her name tag, trying to place her. She looked familiar, but frankly I had no idea where we'd met.

"'We have a seat at our table. Come, join us for lunch,' the woman suggested.

"Following her, I was eager to solve the mystery. When we reached our seats, I glanced at the faces around the table. None of them looked familiar. The woman introduced me to the staff from the publishing house where she'd worked as an editor for several years. She'd also been successfully selling her material. She laughed and said, 'I don't know if you even remember our first meeting. It was at the Christian Writers' Conference in 1989.'

"No wonder I didn't remember who she was, I thought to myself. That was years ago! 'You look familiar,' I replied, 'but to be honest, I've been trying to place you.'

"She paused for a moment, searching for the right words.

"'At that conference,' she told me, 'I had a private appointment with you. You read the story I was working on and advised me to pursue writing. You said if I persevered I'd get published.' She smiled. 'Well, I stuck with it. In time I started selling articles and stories. Now I'm on the editorial side. Whenever I got discouraged, I thought of your encouraging words that Saturday so long ago.'

"As I listened to this woman's story, our previous meeting started to come back to me. 'Yes, I remember you now,' I told her. 'I'm excited to see what you have done with your talent.' I felt a warm glow as we continued to chat.

"After lunch we went our separate ways and I felt encouraged. Although I speak at many conferences and meet with hundreds of would-be writers, it's exciting when God shows me the fruit of my efforts in teaching others to write to glorify him."

It is exciting to see the impact Susan's encouraging words had on a budding writer. And they came back full circle, encouraging her in God's calling on her life! Her story makes us more conscious of the power of words. They are boomerangs that come back to us, for good or bad. We should keep this in mind before carelessly tossing them to others.

Could your encouragement help someone reach goals she has only dreamed about? You'll never know until you apply your expressions of support to the lives of others.

When to Use Encouraging Words

There are many times to apply encouraging words. You may use them to:

- Point a friend in the right direction
- Motivate a friend
- Inspire a friend
- Challenge a friend
- Comfort a friend
- Bolster a friend's confidence.

When you see an opportunity to apply your words to accomplish one of these feats, by all means, do it! The results will be amazing. My friend Karen, a professional seamstress, recently had her confidence bolstered with encouraging words. She'd been making a suit for a grouchy client. At the first fitting, the garment hung loosely across her client's shoulders. As Karen pinned the garment for a better fit, the client cursed her and said, "You're the worst seamstress I have ever worked with."

Later that day, Karen went to pick up her son from school. With tears in her eyes, she shared the incident with another mother whose daughter, Sara Ann, was one of Karen's sewing students. Sara Ann was listening and hugged Karen and said, "I think you're the best seamstress in the world." Karen told me those words helped erase some of the pain.

Karen was able to put the incident into perspective, realizing she was not a bad seamstress but a good seamstress who had simply had a bad day. Karen was able to step across the incident as if she were walking across a bridge, confident she was the professional she was striving to be.

Expressing Encouragement

There are many ways to express encouraging words. You can write them in a letter or e-mail, communicate them through a phone call, record them on video or share them in person. Just as there are several ways to share your encouragement, there are several forms of encouragement. You may wish to use:

- Compliments
- Persuasion
- Congratulations
- Encouragement playback
- Appreciation
- Compliments

A compliment is an expression of approval or admiration. Author Diana L. James tells about the time a compliment made a big impact on her life: "The fifth-graders scurried into the classroom that April morning with eager anticipation. That is, all of them except me. I shuffled to my seat with a sense of hopelessness. For me, it was just another day of feeling inferior. No matter what I did, I felt I could never measure up to the other kids and I knew I could never measure up to my older brother.

"Oh, it wasn't that my brother put me down. He didn't need to; I did it myself. Every time I heard people talk about how smart, how witty, how intelligent my brother was, I knew something was wrong with me. 'Why did David have to get all the brains in the family?' I asked myself.

"As if that weren't enough, he was the one with all the athletic talent too. He could beat anyone at Ping-Pong, darts, basketball and any other sport he cared to try—while

I, on the other hand, couldn't even win at tiddlywinks and my attempts at more physical sports always ended in disaster.

"Not that I wanted to be a boy like my brother. No, actually, I liked being a girl, but I just wanted to be a girl who was good at something—anything!

"Our teacher called the class to order that morning and reminded us to be on our best behavior because the music teacher was coming that day. As if on cue, the door opened and in bounced a young woman with a big smile, an armful of song sheets and a pitch pipe. Mrs. Benson taught us a song, then walked up and down the rows of seats, listening as we tried to sing it without her help. She said, 'Now, I want to hear everyone singing. Come on, boys and girls, a little louder, please.'

"As Mrs. Benson walked up the aisle where I was sitting, she suddenly stopped beside my seat. I froze. I knew I must be doing something wrong—singing the wrong words, the wrong notes or the wrong tempo. I shut my mouth. 'Don't stop, children. Everyone keep singing,' she said.

"Dutifully, I obeyed, hoping Mrs. Benson would move on. She didn't. All at once, I felt her hand on the top of my head. Mrs. Benson spoke, not to me, but to my teacher. 'This one's got a lovely voice. I want her in the Girls' Glee Club,' she said, her hand still resting lightly on my head. I couldn't believe my ears. Was she really talking about ME?

"Suddenly, I felt as if sparklers and fireworks were shooting all over the room. I wanted to shout, dance, hug Mrs. Benson. I felt valuable—something I had never felt before.

"Mrs. Benson changed the direction of my life that April day. With her encouragement, I became a member of the glee club, joined the youth choir at my church and later sang in high school and college a cappella choirs, madrigal groups and church choirs wherever I have lived. Music has brought joy and fulfillment to my life. The hymns I sang even helped lead me to the Lord.

"Mrs. Benson never knew what a lifelong effect her encouraging words had on me. But it's a lesson I try to remember always: We must speak to people, especially children, with words of praise and encouragement. You never know when it might dispel the gloom of hopelessness and open for them a whole new life."

Persuasion

Persuasion is a form of encouragement that can challenge and inspire others. Sometimes all it takes to reach a goal is for someone to come alongside and say, "You can do it! You'll get through it."

Avonne found this kind of help made a big difference in a challenge she encountered. "I was facing a decision about taking a leadership position that seemed overwhelming to me," she said. "A friend told me she felt I was the only one for the job and that God would help me."

With this encouragement, Avonne was persuaded to tackle the new role. She discovered her friend was right and God helped her do it!

Congratulations

It is always encouraging to be recognized for a job well done. Whenever my parents visit from out of state, my mom leaves telling me how well she thinks I'm doing running my home, mothering my children and caring for my husband. It's great to hear those words.

Rona Peace found the "you did its" made a difference in her life. She says, "The first time I played piano for church was because a kind older woman told me, 'You shouldn't be ashamed to play the piano—you have a talent most of us don't have.'

"I was extremely nervous that day and my heart was beating rapidly. Unfortunately, I used my heartbeat as a metronome and what should have been played at a march tempo was played at a runaway gallop. That ended my piano performing days for a long time.

"Years later, after enduring weeks of poor performances by sincere yet incapable pianists at church, I volunteered to share my piano talent once again. Although I was nervous, age had given me the control I needed to get through the selection. When I had finished, there was an uncomfortable silence followed by rare Lutheran church applause. After the service, many parishioners stopped to congratulate me. Later, I was hired as the music director."

Rona did it! The applause and congratulations gave her the encouragement she needed to share her musical talents.

Never forget to let someone know you have noticed what they've accomplished; it could inspire them to use their talent even more.

Encouragement Playback

Although most forms of gossip are hurtful and mean-spirited, I often practice what I call "Encouragement Playback." This means I try to pass along something good someone has said about someone else.

One day I called a friend to congratulate her for a great article she wrote for one of my favorite publications. "Your article was great!" I told her. "Everyone I've mentioned it to has commented on how well it's written."

"Thanks," Angie said. "That makes me feel better. The last article I wrote for that publication got a lot of letters from people who disagreed with me. I was feeling really discouraged."

"Really?" I said. "The editor of the publication told me that you do a great job for her!"

"She said that?"

"Yes."

"Oh, I can't tell you how much better I feel. I needed to know that."

If you hear something good about someone, pass it along. You never know how much someone may need to hear it.

Appreciation

There is nothing like a well-deserved "Thank you!" to encourage someone. One woman was surprised to find a letter from her husband by her breakfast plate. She said, "Joel wrote how much he loved me and appreciated the ways I'd helped and supported him. He said I was a good mother and made his life better. I was touched. I will always cherish that letter."

I bet this woman felt like a million dollars that day. Wouldn't you love to get a letter like that from your spouse, children, boss or coworker? I know I would. But even better, how would your spouse, children, boss, friends or coworkers feel if they got a letter like that from you? What if you took the time to jot a note like this: "Theresa, I just wanted you to know I couldn't ask for a better daughter than you. You're so special to me. I get tears in my eyes when I think about what a beautiful, sweet young lady you're turning out to be."

Or what if your best friend got a note from you like this: "Becka, thank you so much for being there for me. Words can't express how much I value our friendship. You have always listened to me and helped me whenever I needed you."

Perhaps this is the year you will contact all the people who have played an important role in your life. It might be by letter, phone call or in person. Joe Sabah told me how much it meant to him to get a Christmas call from an old friend expressing appreciation for their friendship. Joe said, "It made me feel I wanted to give this gift to somebody else. I decided, instead of Christmas cards this year, I would call all the people who have meant a lot to me and tell them just that."

What a beautiful idea. Is there someone in your life you should thank?

Accept Encouraging Words

I would challenge you to accept all forms of encouragement that come your way. Be careful not to overlook anything. Keep your eyes open and you will find reassurances. When you do, accept them graciously.

When discouragement comes, forgive hurtful words, especially those spoken in the heat of the moment. If you're struggling to let go of hurtful talk, tell God how you feel and ask him to take your pain. Try to put discouraging words into the perspective of love, as an English novelist suggested in the following poem.

Friendship

By Dinah Marie Mulock Craik

Oh,
The comfort—
The inexpressible comfort
Of feeling safe with a person,
Having neither to weigh thoughts,
Nor measure words, but pour them all right
out, just as they are, chaff and grain together,
Certain that a faithful hand will take and sift
them, keep what is worth keeping—
And with a breath of kindness,
Blow the rest
away.

TWELVE

ENCOURAGE FAITH

Do your friends know you are a person of faith? When they have a crisis, are they aware they can come to you for prayer and encouragement? Perhaps you're like a young woman named Heather whose best friend, Sondra, pulled her aside. "Heather," Sondra said. "I want to talk to you about your soul. Do you know God?"

"Don't worry, I'm in the army of the Lord," Heather replied.

Sondra put her hands on her hips. "We've been friends for years. How come I never knew that?"

Heather leaned forward and whispered, "Because I'm in the secret service!"

Don't be like Heather and put your light under a basket. Never be afraid to encourage someone spiritually.

Your friends need a beacon of hope in a dark world. God may have put you in their paths for this reason. Sharing God may not make you the most popular person in your crowd, but it will make you the most helpful, especially in times of crisis. God will bless you in all your attempts to shed the light of his love on others.

The Difference Faith Can Make

Have you ever needed to have your faith boosted? I have. Early into the ordeal following my daughter's accident, I determined it was up to me to build my faith in God so Laura could be healed. One afternoon, I went into Laura's room armed with my Bible, praise music and carefully written "faith" statements describing my goal that God would soon heal her disabilities. I planned to spend time together with God, proving by my prayers, songs and statements that I had enough faith to see Laura rise and walk.

After an hour of earnestly telling God how much I believed for my miracle, I hit a wall. Suddenly, I knew my three-year struggle to carefully craft my faith had been for nothing. I discovered I had no strength left to believe. Bleary-eyed, I realized that after fighting with all my might, I had lost.

I kissed Laura's white cheek and watched her eyelashes flutter open as she fixed her gaze upon the ceiling. The lump in my throat became a knot in my stomach as I tried to continue my petition to God. I turned the onionskin pages of my Bible to yet another faith Scripture, but the blurry print could not give me hope. Sighing, I shut the book. Laura's never going to get better, I anguished as the rain-filled wind blew against her windowpane, saturating my spirit with despair. Our situation is hopeless.

Later, I hid in the darkness of my bedroom, curtains drawn against the cold, relentless drizzle. "Lord," I prayed,

"Are you there? I need you to speak to me if you want me to continue to hope. Please show me what to do."

That evening in church, the thundering voice of my pastor dropped to a low rumble. "The Lord has shown me there is someone here tonight who has lost hope," he said.

I froze in my seat. Goose bumps crawled up my arms. The pastor's eyes searched the hundreds of faces in the congregation, as I tried to appear invisible. "God wants you to look up. He's with you and will restore your hope in him."

I was stunned. This message was too close to be a coincidence. Maybe God is with me, I reasoned.

Driving home, a full moon reflected on the wet roadway, illuminating my thoughts as I turned my attention from myself to God. I began to see I had missed God's truth by placing my faith not in him but in the earthly vessel of myself. I had spent all of my energy trying to have faith in my faith! Like two index fingers trapped in struggle against the woven fibers of a Chinese finger puzzle, I had been held captive by trusting myself instead of trusting God.

I pulled my van into the stillness of my garage as darkness surrendered to the illumination of the ceiling light. Turning off the engine, I laid my head on the steering wheel. "Lord," I prayed, my spirit calming, "I transfer all my faith from myself to you." In my mind's eye, I could see Jesus' loving face as I handed him the limp body of my daughter. "Lord, Laura is yours," I prayed. "I'm going to trust you with her future. My faith in you no longer depends upon her healing." In the words of Job 13:15, I said, "Though he slay me, yet will I trust in him."

In that moment, the weight of despair was lifted off my shoulders. I knew God had answered me. I did not have to try to create hope by myself. Like release won from the Chinese finger puzzle, I no longer struggled against myself but pushed toward God. I was free at last.

In my journey from despair to hope, I've learned faith is not trying to make God do your bidding. Faith is simply knowing God is able, then trusting him with the results. How glad I am I was finally able to see this truth. Since the night of my garage prayer, God has moved on my daughter's behalf. Although still severely disabled, Laura is alert, full of smiles and fun. No, she has not been set free from her wheelchair, but her love knows no bounds. Her life is filled with joy.

How grateful I am my pastor encouraged me with the words, "God wants you to look up. He's with you and will restore your hope in him."

Perhaps you have a friend who needs this kind of encouragement. Perhaps you have a friend who has never met God and needs to be introduced or perhaps you're the one who needs spiritual encouragement. God is waiting for you. He's ready to comfort you and grow a deeper relationship with you. All you have to do is "look up."

When to Encourage the Faith

When might you encourage someone in the faith? Whenever the opportunity arises!

Mimi Deeths wrote to tell me of a time she helped encourage the faith of a friend. She wrote: "Pat was a darling little blonde with spirit and a smile. She, like me, had been diagnosed with colon cancer and we were receiving chemotherapy in the same office. The fact that misery loves company was obvious from the laughter flowing between us the first day we met. Comparing experiences and griping about the undesirable side effects of the medication brought about an automatic sense of camaraderie.

"I confessed to Pat that I worked out some of my frustration by writing a book about my experiences. I mentioned casually that most of the book was still inside my head because I was such a poor typist. Pat laughed and said, 'We'd make a great pair. I'm an executive secretary and I love to type, but I have no ideas for a book of my own. Why don't you tell me your story and I'll type it.'

"So we started. I poured out my feelings about my disease as Pat listened. My story of faith developing through a life-threatening disease interested Pat, then overwhelmed her. Pat said she admired the faith I possessed in the face of adversity and she encouraged me to share more of it with her.

"Over the next year and a half, Pat learned more about the God whom she'd placed behind other priorities in her life. She felt God was angry with her and did not pay attention to her. I assured her that if she began to pray, God would hear her prayers. She returned to church after many years away and her family began to accompany her there. They became united under the embrace of God's love.

"Eventually Pat chose to let God take control of her life. Since then, her cancer has spread. She may not live long, but now she knows how to approach the throne of God."

Later, Mimi wrote me: "It is hard saying good-bye to the special friend I've known too short a time. I have to do the typing myself now, but I'm getting better at it. Yesterday I typed this note to Pat, who is in hospice care, about to be promoted from secretary to saint:

To my dear friend, Pat—

> What do you do when the agony is too much to bear?
>
> Seek God's face and learn to love him more.

He asks no longer that you be his hands reaching out on this earth to do his work.

He invites you now to rest your hands—those hands which prayed and sought his work to do, those little girl's hands with which you once discovered the world around you, the tender arms which held babies and directed little children in the right way to live, the working hands which kept a tidy house, the fast flying fingers which typed so efficiently, the loving hands which provided a ready reach for those in need, the tiny, delicate hands which slip gently into the strong hands of the man you love, the weary hands that reach out and say to loved ones, "I need you near."

Lay your hands to rest now, Pat and seek the face of God. He loves you and you will see the love in his eyes. You are his precious child. He wants to take you to his heart, brave warrior. Your battle is over.

Love, Mimi

When Pat died, Mimi shared her letter of good-bye at her funeral. Since the day Mimi delivered that eulogy those many years ago, Mimi herself has graduated to heaven where she was reunited with both her Lord and her friend. What a day that must have been!

But in the days when Mimi was still earthbound, she was able to share her faith and spiritual encouragement right in the midst of her pain and suffering. It didn't matter if it was in the middle of her own cancer treatment or even that she was wrestling with heartaches of her own. Not only did she not let her own circumstances stop her from reaching out to Pat, she used those circumstances as an excuse to reach out. I'm so proud of Mimi and grateful to her for reminding me to make the best of the opportunities for spiritual encouragement that are all around me.

How to Encourage Faith

The apostle Peter tells us how to share our faith:

> "But in your hearts set apart Christ as Lord. Always be prepared to give an answer to everyone who asks you to give the reason for the hope that you have. But do this with gentleness and respect" (1 Peter 3:15).

I would add to Peter's words, don't hit people over the head with your Bible. Instead, share what God has done for you with words straight from your heart. Faith is personal and you should share it in a loving, personal way. Don't worry about saying the wrong thing. If you're excited about something the Lord has done for you, tell someone. As long as you tell it in love, you can't fail. God will bless your efforts.

Recently I attended a meeting where Glenna Salsbury, past president of the National Speakers' Association, shared her faith in a presentation to a secular audience. I sat in my chair, stunned.

Afterward, I pulled her aside. "Glenna, you just shared your faith from the platform!" I exclaimed.

Her eyes danced. "I know. I simply gave the audience what they wanted to hear. I spoke about my experience."

I thought about Glenna's remark for several weeks.

Later, I was asked to present a talk to a secular group of peers, a group with whom I had nearly caused a riot only weeks before when I had ended the lunch prayer with the words, "in Jesus' name." I knew I was facing the possibility of the same hostility but decided to take Glenna's lead. I decided to share a personal experience of faith combined with a Bible story about Jesus.

I felt nervous as I walked to the front of the room. Were my peers going to label me "one of those religious nuts" and ask me to keep my belief system to myself? Probably, I reasoned.

As I began to speak, I could sense the audience getting caught up in my anecdote about a dramatic answer to prayer. I tied this narrative with the story of Mary wanting to sit at the feet of Jesus as he taught. I was astounded when the group applauded wildly, many dabbing tears from their eyes.

A man who had been avoiding me since the lunchtime prayer incident said, "I liked you and I liked what you said."

A woman said, "Thank you for telling the story about Mary. You made me want to hear more about Jesus."

A young, professing Buddhist agreed. "It was nice to hear something positive about Christ for a change."

A Christian friend encouraged, "See, Linda, you worried for nothing. You didn't offend anyone. You told that story from your heart and the group appreciated it. You gave them something to think about."

I realized I had found the key. Sharing my faith in Christ is most effective when I share my experiences and personal life stories. I could have stood in front of my peers and lectured on the finer points of God's love, but I'm sure they would not have heard me. Instead, when I shared a story that demonstrated God's love, they listened! I was thrilled when one audience member confided, "It was strange. As you talked, I could feel God's love for me!"

Yes! Yes! Yes!

Don't be as afraid as I was to share the stories of your heart. You don't need a podium. A telephone or cup of tea will do. Simply tell your friends what God has done for you.

You may be surprised at how receptive they will be to hear what you have to say. Don't be afraid to repeat yourself. Did you know the average person has to hear the gospel 7.6 times before he or she is ready to believe? This means, if you have shared your faith but haven't gotten the response you were hoping for, you may need to share 6.6 more times.

So, what are you waiting for? Tell your friend a story about a personal moment of faith. And when you confront someone with the truth of the gospel, find a common bond. Explain how your beliefs are alike, then share how they differ. This will keep any arguments at bay.

Once I was in an awkward position lying face down while a therapist massaged my neck.

"I believe God is in all things," she said.

I felt my muscles tense at her New Age approach. I wanted to sit up and argue, but all I could do was listen.

"You see, the universe is God," she explained, going into great detail.

I struggled to keep my neck loose. I prayed silently, "Lord, how can I explain the truth?"

God's inspiration struck me.

"I believe something similar to you," I said finally.

"You do?"

"Yes, I believe God is the force that holds all things together. But the twist is I do not believe I am God. I believe God is in me, because I've asked him, through his Son, to be a part of my life."

The room filled with a stunned silence as the light of truth began to illuminate the therapist's shadows of doubt.

I knew our discussion would resume. It was wonderful to find a point of agreement and point to the truth through it. I hope and pray it will someday lead her to faith in Christ.

I like the question evangelist Bill Fay with whom I wrote Share Jesus Without Fear (B&H) asks after listening to someone's spiritual beliefs: "If you were wrong, would you want to know?"

What a great lead to present the truth of God's love! It takes you out of the role of preacher. You're only asking a question in love. If your friend answers, "No," then you must respect her wish. If she answers, "Yes," then you have her permission to share your faith. In that case, I recommend you pull out your Bible and show your friend the following Scriptures. Have her read them aloud. Ask, "What does this say to you?" Allow her time to think about it.

All have sinned.

> "For all have sinned and fall short of the glory of God" (Romans 3:23).

The wages of sin is death.

> "For the wages of sin is death, but the gift of God is eternal life in Christ Jesus our Lord" (Romans 6:23).

God sent his son to die in our place.

> "For God so loved the world that he gave his one and only Son, that whoever believes in him shall not perish but have eternal life" (Jphn 3:16).

Christ died for our sins.

> "But God demonstrates his own love for us in this: While we were still sinners, Christ died for us" (Romans 5:8).

Through the sacrifice and resurrection of Christ, we can be forgiven our sins and we can know God.

> "Therefore, there is now no condemnation for those who are in Christ Jesus, because through Christ Jesus the law of the Spirit of life set me free from the law of sin and death" (Romans 8:1-2).

Ask, "Are you ready to invite Jesus into your life and heart?"

If she is, lead her in a simple prayer like, "Father, I am a sinner. Please forgive me of my sins. Thank you for sending your Son to die in my place. Thank you that he rose again. I surrender my life to him. In Jesus' name, Amen." If you would like more information on how to share your faith, I recommend the book Share Jesus Without Fear, which Bill Fay and I coauthored.[1]

How to Encourage Your Own Faith

If you want to be encouraged in faith, make sure you know God. For best results, be guided by the following recipe.

Recipe for Becoming New

Cook's Note: This recipe is the delight of the humble in spirit.

Ingredients:

1 Bible

1 open heart

2 knees, bent

1 humble spirit

1 invitation

Directions:

Open the Good Book and read John 3:16. Open your heart. If its hinges are stiff or rusty, pry it open on bent knees. With humble spirit, invite God to make you brand-new.[2]

Once you have asked God, through Jesus, to be the Lord of your life, you need to grow in order to know him more closely. I find prayer—simply talking to God and reading the Bible—most helpful.

Penny Prater agrees. She has relied on Romans 8:28 to encourage her many times: "And we know that in all things God works for the good of those who love him, who have been called according to his purpose."

Are there other Scriptures that will encourage you? Yes, the Bible is full of them. Here are a few of my personal favorites:

For Strength

> "I can do everything through him who gives me strength" (Philippians 4:13).

When Worried

> "Do not be anxious about anything, but in everything, by prayer and petition, with thanksgiving, present your requests to God. And the peace of God, which transcends all understanding, will guard your hearts and your minds in Christ Jesus" (Philippians 4:6-7).

When Confused

> "Trust in the Lord with all your heart and lean not on your own understanding" (Proverbs 3:5).

For Love

> "For this reason I kneel before the Father, from whom his whole family in heaven and on earth derives its name. I pray that out of his glorious riches he may strengthen you with

power through his Spirit in your inner being, so that Christ may dwell in your hearts through faith. And I pray that you, being rooted and established in love, may have power, together with all the saints, to grasp how wide and long and high and deep is the love of Christ, and to know this love that surpasses knowledge—that you may be filled to the measure of all the fullness of God" (Ephesians 3:14-19).

For Peace

"Peace I leave with you; my peace I give you. I do not give to you as the world gives. Do not let your hearts be troubled and do not be afraid" (John 14:27).

For Power

"He gives strength to the weary and increases the power of the weak" (Isaiah 40:29).

Freedom from Anxiety

"Cast all your anxiety on him because he cares for you" (1 Peter 5:7).

For Direction

"For I know the plans I have for you," declares the Lord, "plans to prosper you and not to harm you, plans to give you hope and a future" (Jeremiah 29:11).

For Counsel

"I will instruct you and teach you in the way you should go; I will counsel you and watch over you."(Psalm 32:8).

For Courage

"Have I not commanded you? Be strong and courageous. Do not be terrified; do not be discouraged, for the Lord your God will be with you wherever you go" (Joshua 1:9).

For Hope

"But those who hope in the Lord will renew their strength. They will soar on wings like eagles; they will run and not grow weary, they will walk and not be faint" (Isaiah 40:31).

Now, don't you feel better already?

THIRTEEN

LET GO OF DISCOURAGEMENT

This afternoon, I sat in a coffee shop with Beverly Weston, who lost twin sixteen-year-old daughters in a car accident. As Bev shared about overcoming her tragic loss, she said, "I've learned to pray with an open hand. I say, 'Lord, here's what I want, but I give it to you. Do what you will.'"

This is a profound prayer of faith and trust. By praying this way, Bev is moving toward God. She's letting go of what she never controlled in the first place. She's trusting God, despite pain and loss.

As Bev learned, bad things happen, even to good people. When this realization hits home, it can break our hearts and minds or it can teach us to bend with the storms of life.

Occassionally the Colorado foothills experience early blizzards. The trees which won't bend beneath the weight of the snow or let go of their leaves often break apart. Let's take a lesson from these trees. After all, each of us will face disappointments but when confronted by difficulties, we mustn't stand rigid and unyielding. Instead, we need to bend toward God and let go of our troubles by giving them to him. This process may change us, but it will not break us.

The Difference Yielding Can Make

Letting go can make all the difference, as Nancy Halford, of Louisville, Kentucky, discovered. She said:

In 1992 my husband Rick and I separated after twelve years of marriage. When I married Rick, I married the most sold-out Christian I had ever met. He was giving, loving and intelligent, but most important, he loved the Lord.

I did not recognize the man I left. He was unfaithful to our marriage vows and wasn't sure God existed.

We had a one-year-old daughter and I was six months pregnant with our son. It was difficult for me to leave Rick because I longed for the man I had married and wanted my children to have him as a daddy.

My constant prayer was for Rick to be restored to his faith and to our family. I felt this must be God's will.

While I waited for God to perform this miracle, I cared for our two children and joined a weight loss group at my church.

Every meeting, when we had prayer time, my first request was always for Rick. One night, Lena, a lady whom I respected, spoke after my request. She asked me, "If the Lord showed me something about you, would you want to hear it?"

Of course I said, "Yes!"

Lena said, "God is not punishing you for going against your parents' wishes and marrying Rick. Instead, God is showing great love for you. He is taking care of you. It was his love that brought you back to Louisville to be near your parents. God loves you and wants your children protected from their father's behavior.

"Nancy, you need to concentrate on God's love and not on your expectations that God will change Rick. You should get on with your life as though Rick will never change. Rick has free will and only Rick can make himself be the person he used to be."

At first I was stunned. But after the words had time to sink in, I found great comfort and freedom in them. They gave me the ability to finally let go.

This scene became one of the most encouraging moments during my divorce and recovery.

It has been five years since I left Rick and Rick still has not changed. I still pray for him, but if Rick ever restores his relationship with Christ and with his family, it will be up to him. My life continues in the comfort and freedom of Christ, which Lena helped me see and live.

Nancy was trapped in a state of grief and could not see God's provision. Not only did Lena help Nancy see that God was moving in her life, she helped Nancy see it was time to let go. This does not mean Nancy no longer prays for Rick. Now she prays with an open hand, content to let go and allow God to be in charge of her life.

When to Let Go

How do you know when it's time to let go? I think the answer to that question is whenever you:

Realize you have no control anyway
Seek God's help

'Wait!" you might be saying, "those two conditions describe all my circumstances; I'm not in control and I need to seek God's help!"

Exactly, which is why I wrote:

It's Your Turn, Lord

I found my dream and held it tight,
And prayed for wings to give it flight.
But yet it stayed earthbound with me,
Because I did not set it free.
Although I held it to my heart,
Somehow it seemed to fall apart.
"Oh Lord," I cried unhappily.
"Why did you take my dream from me?"
"My child, your dream is incomplete,
Until you lay it at my feet.
Unless you give your dream to me,
It cannot find its destiny."
I knew I had to let it go,
For I had nothing left to show.
Until my dream was in His hand,
I could not see His plan so grand.
At last I saw what He could do,
He shaped my broken dream anew.
For dreams will never find reward,
Until we say, "It's Your turn, Lord."

How to Let Go

The first step in letting go is to realize you're holding onto something you shouldn't. Sometimes we are like a greedy monkey who has stuck his hand in a small-mouthed jar to steal a banana.

Can't you see this little monkey? He cannot pull his hand out of the jar as long as he's holding the banana and he can't climb up the tree with a glass jar on his hand. But in his little mind he reasons, "I can't let go—the banana belongs to me!"

Is your hand stuck in a jar? What are you holding onto—a broken dream, self-pity, anger, bitterness, despair?

Surprise—your prize is nothing more than a rotting banana. But if you can let go of your prize and give it to God, he can turn it to good. Are you willing to trust him?

You may be thinking, But this thing I'm holding onto is my responsibility. I can't give it to God.

Is that so? Annie Chapman tells of a guidance counselor at her son's school who had this sign posted in her office:

"Do not feel
totally
personally
irrevocably
responsible
for everything.
That's my job.
Love,
God"[1]

You have never owned the thing you have in your hand and you never will. Allow God to pry your fingers off of it so he can move you to the place he longs to take you. Like Nancy, you will be glad you finally let go.

Let Go of Grudges

Don't tell me the thing you have been holding onto is a grudge! Believe me, grudges, bitterness and unforgiveness are the stinkiest of all. Like rotting fruit, others will notice the smell. So what are you waiting for? Isn't it time to let go?

"That's not so easy," you say.

Let's think about it. Letting go of a grudge does not mean the person you forgive deserves your forgiveness. The contrary is probably true. But let me ask you a question. Don't you need to be free of this stench of bitterness? Don't you deserve to be restored to a closer relationship with God? After all, the Lord smells the stench too and he abhors it. He does not abhor you. He loves you but wants you to come clean.

When it comes to forgiveness, Rose Sweet, the author of How to Be First in a Second Marriage, advises that forgiveness is the key to freeing ourselves from bitterness. Rose frequently encourages the women who meet online in the Second Wives online bulletin board. These women from across the country meet daily to share their confusion, hurt and anger over the emotional crises of divided and blended families. In response to these cries for help, Rose says, "We need to conquer the betrayal, anger, hurt, jealousy and bitterness that often last well beyond when the kids grow up and leave home. Hard to do? Yes. Impossible? No. We just need someone to teach us how and that's where the counsel and support from other women help."

Rose said, "The greatest letter of encouragement of God's hope and of his love and grace came to me in this post on the computer bulletin board from a second wife. Here's her story."

Ted and I met at work. I knew he was married, but I didn't care. Our coffee-break chats turned into long lunches, then drives to the beach and ultimately, an affair.

I knew this wasn't right. But somehow I didn't let my guilt stop me. When Jill, Ted's wife, finally discovered our indiscretion, I was relieved. Ted and I were married as soon as their divorce was final.

A couple of years later, Ted and I had a baby of our own. That's when I began to realize how much I must have hurt Jill. Although I was sorry, it was too late. Still, I tried to be a good stepmom to her daughters whenever it was our turn to have the girls in our home.

One day, when my own daughter, Lea, was ten, she and her dad were riding bikes together. I guess Ted never saw the car that hit him. An uninsured drunk driver ended Ted's life in an instant. Ted did not have much life insurance and what he did have went to cover the cost of his burial. Jill, on the other hand, received a huge life insurance settlement as a result of the terms of their divorce.

One day, soon after the funeral, I sat in my kitchen chair, looking over a pile of bills I couldn't pay. I opened a letter from a law firm and found a check for $600 with a note from Jill.

"Louise, I know Ted left you and Lea destitute. Despite the past, I wanted to do something to help. My daughters have told me what a good stepmom you were to them and I know you worked two part-time jobs just so Ted could pay my alimony. Please accept this check and the ones that will follow every month until Lea's eighteenth birthday. Although I prefer no contact from you, please know I have forgiven you. You helped take care of my girls. Now let me help you take care of yours."

This first wife is a woman who no longer has to live with the pain of bitterness. How free she must feel to lay aside her grudge and turn with love and generosity to the woman she once considered an enemy. I applaud this woman's wisdom in letting go. Not just for the sake of the second wife and her ten-year-old daughter but for her own sake as well.

Let Go of Your Expectations

You can't meet everybody's demands. One stressed-out wife, mother and businesswoman complained to her husband about the overload she was experiencing.

"Don't worry about it," he assured her. "You can't do it all, all of the time!"

"Then you won't mind," she quipped, "if I don't bother with trying to be a great wife tonight. I'll sit on the couch and read the paper and try to relax. You start dinner!"

I like this woman's spunk. She's doing what many of us need to do from time to time: delegate. Some women can delegate more easily than others, but regardless of who is washing the dishes and cooking the meals at your house, everyone can better prioritize duties, get rid of busyness and say good-bye to trying to meet every need.

Let Go of Failure

One of the biggest disappointments we may face is failure. But failure is normal. Everyone fails at something, sooner or later. M. H. Alderson said, "If at first you don't succeed, you're running about average."

Some of our greatest heroes could be considered failures. Abraham Lincoln lost his job, was defeated for the legislature, went bankrupt and suffered a nervous breakdown. He was also defeated for speaker of the state legislature, then defeated as an elector of the Presidential Electoral College and lost two bids for Congress. He lost his bid for U.S. Senate and a nomination for the vice presidency. Lincoln was finally elected president in 1860, but by inauguration day, eight states had already seceded from the Union and the nation was on the brink of war. He was eventually assassinated. Yet, think of what this man accomplished: the end of slavery, a fresh start for a nation. A lesser man would have given up long before. Mr. Lincoln did not allow discouragement to defeat him. He kept trying. He kept starting fresh.

Lincoln's story reminds me of what Mary Pickford once said: "You may have a fresh start any moment you choose, for this thing that we call failure is not the falling down but the staying down."

Look for the victory in your so-called failures. Don't let failure stop you in your journey. The apostle Peter wrote:

"In this you greatly rejoice, though now for a little while you may have had to suffer grief in all kinds of trials. These have come so that your faith—of greater worth than gold, which perishes even though refined by fire—may be proved genuine and may result in praise, glory and honor when Jesus Christ is revealed. Though you have not seen him, you love him; and even though you do not see him now, you believe in him and are filled with an inexpressible and glorious joy, for you are receiving the goal of your faith, the salvation of your souls" (1 Peter 1:6-9).

A few summers ago, my husband, son and I were standing on a downhill world-cup bicycle racecourse on a mountain in Vail, Colorado. The racers pointed their bikes down the dirt trail and raced down the winding track. Just as one racer pounded past where we were standing, his bike hit a boulder and broke in half. The rider flew through the air before skidding across the gravel on his hands and knees.

Doesn't this sound like defeat? Here he was, lying in the dirt, a broken bicycle by his side and the finish line only a few feet away. Suddenly the cyclist scrambled to his feet. To the delight of the cheering crowd and rolling TV cameras, he picked up both halves of his bike and ran across the finish line.

Was this young man a loser? His victory was not in winning the race but in finishing the race. Besides, who do you think made CNN Sports that night? The winner of the race got recognized, but it was the young man carrying his broken bike across the finish line who was highlighted.

There are other kinds of victories in defeat. I wrote this poem about victories of love.

Victors

Runners line the starting gate,
Their muscles taut,
Waiting for the signal
To race for the prize.
The gun cracks
And they run.
Their eyes fix ahead
And their hopes set to win.
They race, hearts pounding, legs pumping,
Giving it their all.
Then, the unthinkable . . .
A stumble, a fall.
The crowd holds its breath
Watching the runner plunge,
With hands outstretched
Grasping at air, grasping at gravel.
A fellow runner
Stops his race,
Turns back to reach down
To help a friend.
The crowd cheers
As the pair limps toward the goal
Dead last.
Victors, in every sense of the word.

Prayer of Release

Once you've determined to let go of what you had once gripped so tightly, the question may be, how? I recommend prayer. To pry your fingers off your prize, you may need to pray something like this:

Lord, I release ________ to you. I lay it/him/her at your feet. I ask that you take my prize and turn it into good. If I pick it up again, remind me to let go. Give me strength, courage, grace and mercy. In Jesus' name, Amen.

Congratulations! If you have prayed this prayer, you have started a new adventure with God. You have learned to let go of whatever's been holding you back. You have learned to leave the results to the Lord of the universe. Don't look now, but you're definitely going places you have only dared to imagine. I wish you a wonderful journey.

Fourteen

You Can Do It

One summer day, long before we had children, Paul and I decided to hike into a hidden valley in the Sangre De Cisto mountain range in southern Colorado. This beautiful valley and glassy lake are surrounded by rugged 14,000-foot mountain peaks. We set up our tent at the edge of the wildflower-filled meadow and pine forest, planning the next day's climbing adventures.

Paul was set to climb the magnificent but deadly Crestone Needle with a group of experienced mountaineers. The Needle was a 14,197-foot vertical piece of jagged rock jutting from the earth. It could only be conquered with climbing ropes and crampons. My friend Debbie and I decided to go for the more modest Humboldt Peak. It was a mere 14,064-foot green, rounded orb, complete with hiking path. "Perfect," I decided. "No hanging on ropes for me!"

As Debbie and I began to trudge up Humboldt's steep path, however, I could see the mountain was more challenging than I'd realized. The wind sent a cold chill through my body and the trail was steeper than I'd imagined. I felt if my feet slipped, I would fall forever. Fear conquered me as we neared the boulder field ahead. I froze in my tracks. "I can't go on, Debbie," I admitted. "I feel like I'm going to trip and slide down the mountain."

"Can you walk back down?" Debbie asked.

I swallowed a lump in my throat. "No," I said.

"Can you go up?"

"No, I'm stuck," I admitted.

"Don't worry about it; all you have to do is take another step. Can you do that?"

I nodded. "Yes, I think I can." I took another step and asked, "Now what?"

Debbie said, "Don't worry about it. All you have to do is take another step, okay?"

Slowly, one step at a time, I begin to climb the mountain.

Finally, I made it across the loose boulder fields and crawled my way to the top. The breathtaking view was worth all my effort. Before me lay an ocean of peaks, nestled in billows of fluffy clouds. But best of all, I had overcome my fear!

Sometimes, when you're climbing the mountain of life, there is no gentle voice to coax you to take the next step. Yet, many of the women I talked to felt they needed more encouragement in the following areas:

1. Spiritual Issues
2. Diet and Exercise
3. Christian Living
4. Time Management
5. Child Rearing

6. Housekeeping
7. Marriage
8. Grief
9. Loneliness
10. Job

When you face discouragement in one or more of these areas, there are things you can do to find encouragement. Get inspiration from reading your Bible, listening to Christian radio, reading Christian magazines or books, talking to a friend and praying.

Learn from Your Mistakes

Another way to give yourself a hand is to analyze your struggles. Determine what mistakes you might be making, then decide how you can alter your course. Take a hint from the following short autobiography.

An Autobiography in Five Short Paragraphs

Author Unknown

I walk down the street. There is a deep hole in the sidewalk. I fall in. I am lost. I am helpless. It isn't my fault. It takes forever to find a way out.

I walk down the same street. There is a deep hole in the sidewalk. I pretend I don't see it. I fall in. I can't believe I'm in the same place, but it isn't my fault. It still takes a long time to get out.

I walk down the street. There is a deep hole in the sidewalk. I see it is there. I still fall in. I can't believe I'm in the same place, but it isn't my fault. I get out immediately.

I walk down the street. There is a deep hole in the sidewalk. I walk around it.

I walk down the street. There is a deep hole in the sidewalk. Some poor soul has fallen in. As I help her out, I explain there was a time that used to happen to me. I'm glad to be of assistance.[1]

Do for Others

It is amazing that as you encourage others, you will be encouraged. Ellen says, "I enjoy doing for others. It increases my energy and helps me feel good about myself."

Cassie, a single mom, finds encouragement from serving others. She always volunteers to serve hamburgers at the church on Wednesday nights. It encourages her to see other families interacting in healthy ways and dads talking and laughing with their children.

Despite the problems you're trying to conquer, nothing feels better than helping someone else conquer her own problems.

Don't Compare Yourself with Others

Muster your own encouragement by daring to stop comparing yourself with others.

For example, Joleen felt jealous of Melissa, a gifted school teacher. "Why," Joleen wondered, "does she get all the promotions? I'm stuck teaching sixth grade while she gets a higher-paying administrative job! I'm as good as Melissa. That job should have been mine."

Joleen needs to understand God has called each one of us to be a different hue in his rainbow. We are all originals. No one color is more important than another. Perhaps God has chosen Joleen to influence the children in her classroom, while he has chosen Melissa to influence the teachers and administration. When it comes to God's rainbow, it takes all of us to paint the sky in a dazzling array of colors. We should not be jealous of others for doing their part. After all, we are all on the same team. Let's cheer each other on.

Get a New Perspective

Could it be you feel discouraged because things are not progressing as quickly as you would like? Take a look at Noah. It took him 120 years to build the ark. I think I'd feel a little discouraged about 5 years into the call if I were still wrangling with the planning and zoning commission about my backyard project like Noah was. But then, God's timetable is not my timetable.

Is there something you feel God is calling you to do? Are things taking longer than you think they should? Give yourself a break. God's timetable is perfect. Continue to seek him and he will help you to stay on course. You will not arrive a minute too late.

Perhaps it's not the timetable that's bothering you. Perhaps you need a fresh outlook, like Sherry, a young woman who worked with my aunt.

My aunt was a secretary at a large publishing firm and got to be known as the office mom. During coffee breaks she often heard Jackie, a bright young woman, speak of her husband. "You'd never guess what Johnny has gone and done now," Jackie said one day.

Sherry, another bright young woman, asked, "What? Bought you another diamond?"

"No, he's renting a limo to take me on that getaway weekend at the Sheraton!"

"I saw he sent you roses again," Sherry said.

"Isn't he the sweetest thing?" Jackie gushed.

A few days later, my aunt was talking to Sherry.

"I've had it with my husband, Dan," Sherry said. "He's not like Jackie's husband. Why, he's never sent me roses! And when I approached him about hiring a limo for a getaway weekend, he just laughed. I don't know if I can stay married to a man who has such little regard for my feelings."

My aunt said, "Have you really ever considered Dan?"

"What do you mean?" Sherry asked.

"Well, he's so handsome," Aunt Kate said. "Plus, he's a hard worker—working two jobs to take care of you and the boys. I've never seen a man who loved his wife and family more than your husband loves his."

"I know you're right," Sherry said. "But he never wants to do any of the things Jackie's husband does for her."

"Well, after working two jobs that require hard manual labor, I guess he has a hard time parting with his money," my aunt said. "Besides, Jackie's husband knows he has to keep her entertained in order to keep her. But aren't you deeper than that? Besides, think about Jackie's husband's flaws."

Sherry wrinkled her nose.

"Would you really want to be married to him? Wouldn't you rather be married to Dan?"

Sherry sighed. "No question, I'd stick with Dan in a heartbeat!"

"Well, if I were you," my aunt said, "I would concentrate on Dan's good qualities and not think about how he does not do the things Jackie's husband does."

A few weeks later, my aunt was at an office party when Dan and Sherry approached her.

"Hon," Dan asked, "is this the lady who helped turn you around about our marriage?"

Sherry nodded and smiled up at her husband as he put his arm around her. Dan turned to my aunt. "I sure want to thank you," he said.

Sometimes the good or bad of your situation depends on how you look at it. Ask God to help you see your circumstances through his eyes. You may more clearly see the truth.

Make a List

Bonnie Skinner, a speaker and conference director from San Antonio, Texas, created a list of her accomplishments to help boost her confidence. She says, "My ministry began ten years ago when I started women's weekend retreats in my own home. About an hour before my first endeavor, I rested on the living room couch. Everything seemed to be in order and ready for the ladies. At that moment, something incredible happened to me. It was as if the devil sat down beside me and whispered, 'What makes you think you can lead this retreat? These women are going to see right through you. What credentials do you have?'

"The more I thought about this, the more doubt entered my mind. Yes, I thought, what makes me think I can keep a houseful of ladies interested in what I have to say? I'd prepared outlines, posters and colorful folders with handouts to give the ladies. I was ready! But doubt kept rearing its ugly head and soon my confidence and self-esteem began to erode.

"That day I began writing down positive things that had happened to me throughout my life, things that were good or humorous. Gradually, the list grew. It has provided much encouragement through the years. Now, one of my rules is to have at least one success every day; something I can add to my Victory Log. I encourage you to do the same!

Some of my (Bonnie's) humorous entries follow:

- Healthiest 4-H Club girl in our county one year; rode float in the governor's parade.
- Walked down the Washington Monument as high school senior.
- Homecoming Queen in college.
- Collected dry cleaning in my college dorm to earn money.

- Typed church bulletins for two churches weekly during my college years.
- Trimmed ladies' hair while husband was a college student and we had two children.
- Graduated from college in three years.
- Sewed my own clothes for many years.
- Played bridge with astronauts' wives when my husband worked at NASA.
- Sang in church choirs all my life.
- Played piano for NASA Rotary Club for seven years.
- Spit off the Eiffel Tower!
- Met President and Mrs. Carter.

Sometimes we need to write down a list of our accomplishments, including the times when God has rescued us and remembrances of troubles we have overcome. Otherwise, we soon forget we have a history of achievements and answered prayer.

Toss Out the Can'ts

In *Chicken Soup for the Soul*, Chick Moorman tells a story about a unique funeral in "Rest in Peace: The 'I Can't' Funeral."

Donna, a fourth-grade teacher, had her thirty pupils make a list of "I Can'ts":

- "I can't kick the soccer ball past second base."
- "I can't do long division with more than three numerals."
- "I can't get Debbie to like me."

When the children finished their lengthy lists, they folded them in half, brought them to the front of the room and placed them in a shoe box.

Donna led the entire class to the playground, where she proceeded to conduct a eulogy for the "I Can'ts." She told the students, "We have provided 'I Can't' with a final resting place. He is survived by his brothers and sister, 'I Can,' 'I Will,' and 'I'm Going to Right Away.'"[2]

Perhaps you, like the children in Donna's classroom, need to celebrate the death of "I Can't." If you haven't buried him yet, here's your chance.

Make a list of all the "I Can'ts" in your life:

1.
2.
3.
4.
5.
6.
7.
8.
9.
10.
11.
12.
13.
14.
15.
16.
17.
18.
19.
20.

Before we 'bury' this list, please note that we need to have weaknesses before God's strength can be realized. In fact, the apostle Paul wrote:

But he said to me, "My grace is sufficient for you, for my power is made perfect in weakness." Therefore I will boast all the more gladly about my weaknesses, so that Christ's power may rest on me" (2 Corinthians 12:9).

We must never forget we have access to God's power. Paul says: "I can do everything through him who gives me strength" (Phil 4:13).

This means, yes you can! Take another look at your "I Can't" list. This is now your "I Can Through Christ" list. Look at each entry and repeat, "Yes I can through Christ!"

Dare to Dream

If you don't have a dream or goal for which to reach, you'll never go far. Last October, I was in Petaluma, California, inside Jim Groverman's corn maze. Every year, Mr. Groverman takes an acre of corn and creates a walking maze next to his pumpkin patch.

I was amused to watch people wander through the maze as if they knew where they were going. There was no hint in their faces that they were totally lost. My method of seeking freedom was to leave markers of crossed corn cobs along the path. That way if I continued to stumble across one, I would know I was going around in circles.

I watched a man, probably an engineer, make a careful map of where'd he'd been. Yet no one in the maze had a map of where to go. Still, we all had one destination in mind. We were all looking for a way out. And believe it or not, despite our methods or lack thereof, every one of us eventually made it back to the parking lot.

Do you have a destination, dream or goal in mind? Perhaps you want to be the best wife, mother, employee, business owner, writer or whatever that you can be. You must decide where you're going or you will never get there. You need to establish markers along your way, so you can look back and see your progress.

It's a lot like climbing a mountain. As you climb higher on the mountainside, you may not be able to see the top, but you will be able look back to see how far you've come.

Now for the million-dollar question. If you could do anything, what would it be?

Write your dream here:

Give this dream to God; give him permission to take it or to dream it for you. Then, with your dream in mind, turn it into a goal and take it one step at a time.

You Can Do It

Don't believe for one minute you can't reach your God-driven dreams and goals. I dreamed I could write a book about encouragement. Do I really have anything to say? I wondered. OK, I decided, I wouldn't know until I tried. So when I sat down to write this dream and looked at my blank computer screen, fear knotted my stomach. "I can't possibly write a whole book," I thought. I took a deep breath. "Yes I can. God is with me."

I winged off a quick prayer: "Help me, Lord!"

Suddenly, I got an idea and my fingers began to type—one word at a time. That day I typed during my allotted writing time, one hour at a time, then one day at a time, followed by one week at a time and one month at a time, until I reached this final chapter.

And as I look at you, I notice that by your reading this book one page at a time, you have reached this same conclusion; God is with you and he will help you through whatever valley, whatever mountain, whatever calling he has placed on your life, one step at a time.

Sure, there will be plenty of bumps along the way. But maybe that's a good thing as Warren W. Wiersbe described in this story: "A little boy was leading his sister up a mountain path and the way was not too easy. 'Why, this isn't a path at all,' the little girl complained. 'It's all rocky and bumpy.'

"Her brother replied, 'Sure, the bumps are what you climb on.'"[3]

What do you do with the bumps on the path of life? I say, use them as stepping stones and never give up!

Don't Quit

Author Unknown

When things go wrong, as they sometimes will,
When the road you're trudging seems all uphill,
When the funds are low and the debts are high,
When you want to smile, but you have to sigh,
When care is pressing you down a bit,
Rest if you must, but don't you quit.
Life is queer with its twists and turns,
As every one of us sometimes learns,

And many a failure turns about,
When you might have won, if you'd stuck it out.
Don't give up, though the pace seems slow.
You might succeed with another blow.
Often the goal is nearer than
It seems to a faint and faltering man.
Often the struggler has given up
When he might have captured the victor's cup.
And he learned too late when the night slipped down
How close he was to the golden crown.
Success is failure turned inside out,
The silver tint of the clouds of doubt,
And you never can tell how close you are.
It might be near when it seems afar.
So stick to the fight when you're hardest hit.
It's when things seem worst that you mustn't quit.[4]

In your life's journey, you will find ruts along the way. Don't get stuck; seek God to help you rise above your obstacles. As you do, if you see anyone else who is caught in a pitfall, loan them a wing and together, you will soar.

Happy flying and God bless!

Bios

Alene Betts is a toy designer, speaker and author. Child abuse prevention is the platform that brings her many honors.

Beverly Weston is a speaker, trainer and self-image consultant with a unique and compelling story. Beverly shares the importance of image and self-esteem while working through life's challenging transitions.

Bonnie Skinner is a speaker, an author of a manual on women's ministries and served as a staff member of Florence Littauer's CLASSeminar. She and her husband live in San Antonio.

Carolyn R. Scheidies' has written may wonderful novels including her medieval romance *Black Hawk's Feather* which was once voted the fourth-favorite Heartsong historical novel of the year. Scheidies also publishes poetry, devotions, features, articles, short stories and program material.

Diana L. James is a freelance writer and Christian speaker. She's served as compiler, editor and participating author of *Bounce Back and You Can Bounce Back, Too,* both published by Horizon Books.

Dianne E. Butts, a full-time freelance writer and has written for both Christian and secular publications. In her spare time she enjoys photography, motorcycling and movie making.

Karen O'Connor is an award-winning author of *Getting Old Ain't for Wimps* and other bestselling books.
Kathy Collard Miller is a speaker and the author of more than thirty books, including her bestselling *God's Vitamin "C" for the Spirit* and *God's Abundance*.

LeAnn Thieman is an author and professional speaker. Her presentations inspire us to truly live our priorities and balance our lives physically, mentally and spiritually while making a difference in the world.

Lynette Pickering—"Encouragement with a laugh and a song." Known for her transparency and zest for life, Lynette will take you on a journey of sidesplitting laughter with her parodies, "Climb Laundry Mountain" and "I'm Just a Shopper Who Can't Say No."

Mimi Deeths was a wife and mother of four children. She resided in Bakersfield, California where she enjoyed family gatherings when her kids returned from various university campuses for a home-cooked meal. She also brought a unique perspective to cancer patients and their families.

Pam Bianco is a freelance writer and speaker. She and her husband, Steve, have three children and she's involved in a cell-church ministry in Nevada.

Lynne Beaulieu has worked in the information management field for the last thirty-three years. She writes, dances, sews and quilts and is an avid reader. She lives with her cat in California.

Rose Sweet is a popular speaker and author who encourages couples through divorce and remarriage issues.

Susan Titus Osborn has authored several books and numerous articles, devotionals and curriculum materials. Susan is a publisher's representative and teaches at writers' conferences across the United States and internationally.

NOTES

FIVE: Hugs to Embrace

1. Billy Graham, *Just As I Am* (Minneapolis: Billy Graham Evangelistic Association, published by HarperCollins Worldwide, 1997).

SIX: Ears to Hear

1. Anne Rosberger, in "Helping Friends through the Deep Waters of Grief" by Linda Shepherd, Virtue Magazine, September/October 1994, 44.

2. Glen W. Davidson, in *Understanding the Death of the Wished-For Child*, 1979, OGR Service Corp, from "Helping Friends Through the Deep Waters of Grief" by Linda Shepherd, Virtue Magazine, September/ October 1994, 44.

3. H. Norman Wright, in "Helping Friends through the Deep Waters of Grief" by Linda Shepherd, Virtue Magazine, September/October 1994, 44.

4. Linda Shepherd, *Love's Little Recipes for Friendship* (Sisters, OR: Multnomah, 1997), 91.

5. Shepherd, *Love's Little Recipes for Friendship*, 80.

SEVEN: Advice Speaks

1. Richard C. Halverson, "Bullets or Seeds," in *Stories for the Heart*, compiled by Alice Gray (Sisters, OR: Multnomah, 1996), 104.

EIGHT: Relief for Grief

1. Linda Mauer, in "Helping Friends through the Deep Waters of Grief" by Linda Shepherd, Virtue Magazine, September/October 1994, 44.

2. James Dobson, *When God Doesn't Make Sense* (Carol Stream, IL: Tyndale, 1993), 152.

3. Joel Ehrlich, in "Helping Friends through the Deep Waters of Grief" by Linda Shepherd, Virtue Magazine, September/October, 1994, 44.

4. Linda Shepherd, *Love's Little Recipes for Life* (Sisters, OR: Multnomah, 1997), 40.

NINE: Turn for Good
1. Ruth Smeltzer, in *Brilliance: Uncommon Voices from Uncommon Women,* compiled by Dan Zadra with Susan Carlson (Edmonds, WA: Compendium, 1995), 68.

ELEVEN: Nice Words
1. Florence Littauer, *Silver Boxes* (Nashville, TN: Word, 1989), 2-4.

TWELVE: Encourage Faith
1. Bill Fay with Linda Evans Shepherd, *Share Jesus Without Fear* (Nashville, TN: Broadman and Holman, 1999).

2. Shepherd, Love's Little Recipes for Friendship, 63.

THIRTEEN: Let Go of Discouragement
1. Annie Chapman, *Smart Women Keep It Simple* (Minneapolis: Bethany, 1992), 173.

FOURTEEN: You Can Do It!
1. Adapted from *Stories for the Heart,* compiled by Alice Gray (Sisters, OR: Multnomah, 1996), 110.

2. Paraphrased from Chick Moorman, "Rest in Peace: The 'I Can't' Funeral," in *Chicken Soup for the Soul,* compiled

by Jack Canfield and Mark Victor Hansen (Deerfield Beach, FL: Health Communications, 1993), 156.

3. Warren W. Wiersbe, *The Bumps Are What You Climb On: Encouragement for Difficult Days* (Grand Rapids, MI: Baker, 1984).

4. Adapted from Willie Jolley, *It Only Takes a Minute to Change Your Life* (New York: St. Martin's, 1997), 106.

About Linda Evans Shepherd

Linda has published thirty books, including her bestselling 'When You Pray Series, including *When You Need a Miracle -- How to Ask God for the Impossible* and *When You Don't Know What to Pray – How to Talk to God About Anything*. She's the author behind the perennial bestseller, *Share Jesus Without Fear*. She's also the creator of the bestselling novel series, *The Potluck Club* and *The Potluck Catering Club*, which she co-wrote with Eva Marie Everson. She's been named a top-ten Crossings author and is a proven Choice Books favorite. She's a Carol Award winner and her book *When You Can't Find God* won the 2012 Selah Award for Christian Life.

Christian Retailing compares Linda to both Beth Moore and Stormy Omartian while John DeBrine, the host of the radio show *Songtime USA*, said Linda reminds him of a little lady he met in the sixties by the name of Corrie ten Boom.

Patsy Clairmont says, "There is a bubbling up of Jesus-Joy that exudes from Linda that is absolutely contagious. I love her blend of humor and heart and I stand back amazed at her "go tell the world" determination.

Linda has empowered thousands across North America and Europe to release their burdens to God and to walk closer with him. Her online and speaking ministries have seen over 300,000 people come to faith.

Linda has spent her life trying to focus on God, even despite tragic circumstances. Linda saw God help her turn the "pits" of her life into stepping stones following a car crash that left her then infant daughter in a year-long coma before she awoke. Today, Linda's daughter is 25-years-old and Linda is a respected women in Christian ministry. She's the President of Right to the Heart Ministries which oversees the work of AWSA (Advanced Writers and Speakers Association) and GodTest.com as well as the blogs www.FindingGodDaily.com and www.ThinkingAboutSuicide.com and is the founder of www.FabulousSpeakers.com.

She's been married over thirty years to Paul and has two young-adult children, Laura and Jimmy.

To learn more about Linda's books and speaking ministry, go to: www.GotToPray.com

9676695R00109

Made in the USA
San Bernardino, CA
23 March 2014